Distributed
Database
Management
Systems

Lexington Books Series in Computer Science
Kenneth J. Thurber, General Editor

Distributed Database Management Systems

Olin H. Bray
Control Data Corporation

LexingtonBooks
D.C. Heath and Company
Lexington, Massachusetts
Toronto

Library of Congress Cataloging in Publication Data

Bray, Olin H.
  Distributed database management systems.

  Bibliography: p.
  Includes index.
  1. Data base management.   2. Electronic data processing—Distributed
processing.   I. Title.
QA76.9.D3B712   001.64   79–3184
ISBN 0–669–03396–0   AACR2

Second printing, October 1983

Published simultaneously in Canada

Printed in the United States of America

International Standard Book Number: 0–669–03396–0

Library of Congress Catalog Card Number: 79–3184

Contents

List of Figures

Foreword

Discussing distributed database management has turned out to be as difficult as doing it. Problems and solutions emerge piecemeal from the ferment of the research pot, stimulated by the heat of the promise of cheaper hardware. Where response can be improved by parallel hardware, distribution in the form of parallel processes is an enticing concept.

However, coordination and control cast an ever larger shadow both on the achievement of distribution and on the discussion of its promise. In these discussions of distributed database, the multitude of separate groups in both hardware and software for both database management and communications have produced a massive clamor that resists coordination.

It is time for an overview with a defined perspective. Indeed, it is time for a number of overviews to bring out the perspectives of the various active groups so that the variations of the promise, the risks of unsolved problems, and the paradoxes of unresolved interfaces can be fully aired and overcome.

This book describes from a software perspective the challenge that distributed database throws down to proponents of distributed computing. It notes the diversity of efforts (displayed at length in the bibliography). The coordination of these disparate efforts, their marketing motivations and technical biases, can be achieved by our market economy only with the aid of public discussion. This discussion must illuminate the needs for and objectives of distributed database, the computing and communication capacities to support its objectives, and the software to convert language and data to bits and bytes and bring them back again as information—where it's needed, with reliability and security as well as speed and economy.

On with the discussion.

William H. Stieger
Chairman,
CODASYL Systems Committee

Preface

Distributed database and *distributed database management* are two terms that are being heard with increasing frequency. In some cases these terms are applied to very sophisticated experimental systems, but in other cases they are used to refer to relatively simple enhancements of current centralized database management systems. Furthermore, much of the current research work focuses on relatively narrow, specific technical problems. These problems are important and must be solved. However, before an organization moves into the distributed database area, it should consider the approach from a broad overall perspective. What are the objectives to be accomplished? What are the alternatives, if any, to distributed processing and distributed database management? If the distributed database approach is selected, what are the various alternatives and the implications of each? Only at this point can the results of much of the current research activity become meaningful to the practitioner.

This book attempts to provide this broader perspective. It begins by considering database management and data communications. It then describes a series of distributed-processing alternatives, of which distributed database management is the most complicated. It goes on to discuss the basic concepts of distributed database management and its various distribution alternatives. Finally, it describes and relates the various technical issues, such as data placement and update synchronization, on which most of the current research is being done.

No book is solely the work of one person. Many people are working in the distributed database area, and the results of much of their research are reflected in this book. I would especially like to thank the other members of the CODASYL Systems Committee with whom I have had many valuable discussions over the past four years. These discussions have significantly improved the quality of the book. I would also like to thank Jan Bray for her extensive help in editing parts of the book. Finally, I would like to thank Mary Ellen Lifson for her help in typing the manuscript.

1 Introduction

With so many books, journals, and research reports in the data processing and computer science area, every author should ask himself whether another is necessary? What is the purpose of this book that others do not already accomplish? In this case, there is a very specific purpose and target audience.

This book is intended as a concise but readable introduction to the concepts involved in distributed database management. It should help the reader understand the basic issues involved in designing a distributed database management system and the applications that must use such systems. This book does not attempt to provide the definitive answer for distributed database management. Indeed, in many areas there is so far no such answer. In these areas, the book identifies the major issues and trade-offs, describes the current state of the art, and suggests a direction for future research that may some day provide more definitive answers. For those who wish to pursue a specific area in more detail, there is an extensive bibliography.

This book will not make the reader an expert in distributed database management, but it provides a beginning by introducing all the basic concepts and showing how the various technical issues are related. After completing this book, the reader should understand how the various parts of distributed database management fit together and should be able to read and understand much of the technical literature.

This book has three specific target audiences. First, it is directed to many of the database practitioners who are now being forced to consider many of the issues discussed here. Many, although not all, are experienced in database management in a centralized system. However, because of technological developments, they now need to understand how these concepts must be enhanced to remain applicable in a distributed environment. The second group is the data communications and distributed processing practitioners who are now beginning to see serious data management problems and must determine how database management concepts can help them. Also, communications requirements may be very different when the communication is between complex database management systems, rather than special application programs. An example of this type of problem occurs in the layered architecture proposed by the International Standards Organization (ISO) for open systems interconnections.[1] Except for the application and presentation layers, all the functional layers involve only communications. It is not clear that all the distributed database management system functions can be performed adequately at the application layer.

The third important audience is the computer science and management information systems students. For them this book can provide a bridge for integrating the concepts of distributed processing and those of database management. The extensive bibliography will be especially valuable for this last group.

The book is organized into ten chapters and a bibliography. Chapter 2 discusses database management in a centralized system—that is, as it is done today. It describes the objectives of database management, its components, and its operations. Part of the chapter focuses on database management systems in general, but there are separate sections that specifically discuss CODASYL or network systems and relational systems. There is also a section that addresses the commonality of the two approaches and ways of mapping from one type of system to the other.

Chapter 3 provides a comparable introduction to data communications. Distributed database management requires some background in both database management and data communications. Therefore, these two chapters attempt to ensure that all the readers have at least a minimum background in both areas. This chapter discusses some basic communications concepts, identifies several key technologies, and reviews the open systems interconnection architecture proposed by the ISO.

Chapter 4 considers distributed processing in general. It discusses the benefits and limitations of distributed processing and identifies a variety of distribution alternatives. The last alternative is a distributed database management system. This leads directly into chapter 5, which identifies and explains the various concepts of distributed database management. Many of the concepts discussed in this chapter were developed by the CODASYL Systems Committee in their latest report, *A Framework for Distributed Database Systems: Distributed Alternatives and Generic Architecture.*[2] The chapter identifies the components of a distributed database management system (DDBMS), explains its operations, discusses four types of distribution, and shows how these can be applied to each of the components.

Each of the next four chapters focuses on a specific area of concern for distributed database management. These issues are data placement, function placement, update synchronization, and request decomposition. None of these areas has general solutions that are appropriate for all types of distributed database systems. Therefore, each chapter identifies the major issues, reviews the current research in the area, and provides some indication of the remaining problems. Chapter 7, "Function Distribution," is a key chapter because it discusses an issue that until now has been considered only in the CODASYL report. Almost all the other work in the area assumes that there is a complete DDBMS at every node in the network.

The final chapter discusses some administration issues and makes some projections about future DDBMS developments. The book concludes with a bibliography that will assist anyone who needs more detailed information on specific areas.

Notes

1. International Organization for Standardization (ISO), *Open Systems Interconnection—Basic Reference Model,* ISO/TC 97/SC 16 (November 1980).

2. CODASYL Systems Committee, *A Framework for Distributed Database Systems: Distributed Alternatives and Generic Architectures* (New York: Association for Computing Machinery, 1981).

2   Database Management Systems

Database management systems allow an organization to improve the use and control of its data resources. Thus, such systems are an important tool for improving the productivity of data processing personnel. They free the applications analysts and programmers from many routine data management concerns. In many organizations this significantly reduces the resources and time required for the development of new applications and the maintenance of existing ones.

This chapter reviews the basic concepts of database management and provides the necessary data management background for the later chapters, which focus on the more technical aspects of distributed database management systems. The reader who is already familiar with database management and with the CODASYL and relational data models may only skim this chapter as a quick review and to ensure a familiarity with all the terms and concepts that are used in later chapters. The reader who is less familiar with database management and with the two data models should understand the terms and concepts introduced in this chapter before proceeding. These concepts are essential to understanding the distributed database environment.

This chapter consists of six sections. Section 2–1 discusses the objectives of database management. Section 2–2 briefly reviews the evolution of database management systems from two distinct types of systems into a single type, and section 2–3 identifies the key components of a database management system (DBMS), and describes how these components function in the actual operation of a DBMS.

The purpose of the chapter is not to describe specific DBMSs but, rather, to explain a general set of functions so that the reader becomes familiar with database management systems in general. Therefore, section 2–3 discusses the components and operations of a DBMS at a general level. This discussion applies to all DBMSs regardless of their type or of the data model on which they are based. Sections 2–4 and 2–5 concentrate on two specific types of DBMSs—the CODASYL and the relational. Section 2–4 discusses the basic terms and concepts of a CODASYL DBMS and describes the basic operation of such a system. Section 2–5 provides a similar introduction to the terms and concepts of a relational DBMS. Later chapters discuss the distribution of both types of systems. Because there is so much discussion and debate about these two data models, section 2–6 makes it clear that they are similar in practice and that it is possible to convert from one to the other and thus allow different users to view a single database in terms of either model.

2-1. Database Management Objectives

The basic goal of database management is to allow an organization to improve its use and control of its data resources. This goal can be divided into four distinct objectives: (1) ease of use; (2) evolvability; (3) data integrity; and (4) data security. Data manipulation or query languages and data independence are two of the main techniques used to meet these objectives. These two techniques, however, are simply means of accomplishing objectives, not objectives in and of themselves. Specific DBMSs are designed to meet these four objectives to varying degrees. Two types of design trade-offs occur. First, there are trade-offs among objectives. For example, ease of use may be emphasized at the expense of improved security. Second, there are trade-offs between the extent to which these functional objectives are met and the computer performance of the DBMS. Each of these objectives is discussed later in more detail.

Ease of Use

The first objective is to make the DBMS easy to use. If the system is hard to use, people will need more training time and will make more mistakes. As a result, fewer people will be able to use the system directly. If the end users are unable to use the DBMS directly, then all their requests will have to go through the programming staff. This will increase the programmer's workload and lengthen the time required to develop an application or answer a user's question. Ease of use is important because of the relative costs of hardware and software. Although the high-level query languages required to provide this ease of use, especially for the nonprogramming end user, are less machine efficient, they do allow the expensive data processing personnel to use their time more efficiently. The computer and the DBMS are doing some of the work that was previously done by analysts and programmers. Considering the rapid decline in hardware costs and the increase in personnel costs without offsetting improvements in productivity, this is a reasonable trade-off. Although the power and flexibility of query languages vary among different DBMSs, all DBMSs provide some support for this ease-of-use objective.

This ease of use should be provided to both the programmer and the nonprogrammer end user. Many DBMSs provide a self-contained high-level query language for the end user. With this type of language the user needs to specify only what data is desired, not how to obtain it. Since the database has been previously defined, the DBMS can analyze the request to determine how to obtain the data. Ideally, this type of capability should also be provided to the programmer. In many systems, however, the data manipulation language used by the programmer is at a much lower level. Even this low-level data manipulation language provides some benefits for the programmer, but it has nowhere near the power and flexibility of the end user's query language. For example, a high-level query request might ask for all the orders for a particular customer. To get the same data, the programmer normally would have to identify the customer first and then retrieve the related orders one at a time.

Evolvability

Evolvability is, in a sense, long-term ease of use. It should be easy to modify the database and the applications that use it to meet new or changing requirements. This is an important objective because of the high costs of program maintenance. When an application is initially designed and developed, all its ultimate requirements cannot be clearly defined. Later the application needs to be changed, sometimes because of mistakes in its original design, but often simply because new requirements have emerged since it was developed. In other cases applications that were not cost effective initially become feasible because of changes in hardware or software technology. Evolvability provides a way to change the database to allow new applications or enhancements to old ones without modifying or reprogramming all the existing applications.

Data independence is often used to provide evolvability. This data independence is provided by initially defining the database to the DBMS. Most current DBMSs have two levels of database definition. The first level, the *schema,* provides a complete logical and physical description of the entire database as it is stored. The second level of definition, the *subschema,* provides a logical and formatting description of that part of the database used by a specific application. A database can have only one schema, but there may be a separate subschema for every application. The DBMS uses the schema and the subschema to map data from their stored form to the form that the application expects. This discussion assumes the current two-level database architecture. The three-level or three-schema architecture now being considered by CODASYL is discussed in section 2-3.

Consider the difference between a file system and a DBMS. If a field is added to a record in a file system, the application program must be changed because the record is no longer stored in the same format in which it is described in the application. Since the format of the record is defined only within the application, every application that uses the file must be modified. With a DBMS the stored form of the database is defined in one place, the schema. Only the application that needs the new field is affected. All the other applications are unaffected as long as the DBMS can still map the data from their new stored form into the format the applications expect.

The ability of the DBMS to map data drastically reduces the application maintenance effort. An application must be modified only when the database is changed in such a way that the DBMS can no longer automatically map the data between the forms described in the schema and the subschema. Maintenance is reduced since the only applications that need to be modified are those whose subschema can no longer be mapped from the schema. This mapping does require additional processing and storage overhead. However, considering the cost trade-offs between hardware and software development and maintenance, evolvability is well worth the added hardware costs.

Data Integrity

Improved data integrity is the third DBMS objective. Data integrity has three parts: validity, concurrency, and backup and recovery.

Validity. Validity involves ensuring that only acceptable data values are entered into the database. This guarantees that the value conforms to the database definition, not that it is accurate. In a file system each application is responsible for the integrity of the data it uses. Since the file system knows very little about the data, it can do little integrity checking. In a database system, however, the schema provides a relatively complete definition of the database. Anything that is defined in the schema is known to the DBMS and can be automatically maintained. Moving these editing and integrity checking functions from the application into the DBMS also improves the productivity of software development personnel because in many applications these types of functions are a significant part of the total application.

Concurrent Updates. The second aspect of integrity concerns concurrent updates. Multiple users can access the database at the same time. In most cases this creates no problem. However, if two or more users attempt to modify the same data at the same time, then some of the changes will be lost, and the database will become inaccurate and possibly invalid. To prevent this, the DBMS must control how users are accessing the database. This control of concurrent updates is an important part of the integrity function and must be built into the DBMS because the concurrent users do not know of each other's existence and therefore cannot completely manage the concurrency control within their own programs. This is particularly true for the nonprogramming end user, who does not even realize that such a problem can arise, much less how to deal with it.

Backup and Recovery. Backup and recovery is the third important part of integrity. The DBMS must be able to correct and restore the database when there has been a hardware or software failure. With earlier file systems with multiple generations of the file, recovery was relatively easy. A backup copy of the file was loaded, and the application was rerun. For various reasons (for example, multiple users simultaneously updating different parts of the database, or updates being made directly to the database rather than by creating a new generation of the file) different backup and recovery procedures are required in a DBMS. As with concurrency, the DBMS rather than the individual users of the system must deal with this problem.

Data Security

The fourth DBMS objective is improved data security. The database is a valuable organizational resource that must be protected from unauthorized access and use. An unauthorized access attempt may be the result of an innocent mistake, such as a keying error. On the other hand, it may represent a deliberate attempt to penetrate the system. The type of data and how they can be used determine the amount of security that should be built into the DBMS. Most DBMSs provide a variety of ways to control access to the data. Passwords are one commonly used method. A user must have the proper password to enter the system. Other passwords may be required to access specific parts of the database, such as specific record types or even specific fields within records. A further refinement is to control the operations that can be done on the data once it has been accessed. One password may allow a user to access a particular record type, but a different password may be needed to modify the record. In this way, many users may be allowed to retrieve a certain record type, but only a few may be allowed to update the record, and an even smaller group may be allowed to add or delete records.

Security access controls involving data items and operations can be defined when the database is created and can be checked by examining the user's request and the database definition. There is, however, another type of access control that can be checked only after the DBMS has obtained the data, but before they have been passed to the user. This *value-based security* means that a user may or may not be allowed access to a specific record depending on the data values actually stored in the record. This type of security is often used to prevent violations of privacy. For example, a manager may be allowed to see an employee's salary only if he or she is the manager for that employee. In this case the DBMS may actually have to retrieve the record to determine whether the user is authorized to access it. Value-based security can be used in addition to the more common data-item and operation type of security. In other words, if the user is not a manager, he or she may not be allowed to see any employee records (data-item security), in which case the record would not have to be retrieved.

Some DBMSs also allow *data encryption,* which provides an added level of insurance. If the system is penetrated, the data are meaningless unless the penetrator also knows how they were encrypted. In the past, encryption has been relatively rare in the commercial environment. However, three factors should increase its use significantly in the future: the growing concern with data privacy; the existence of a federal encryption standard; and the availability of encryption hardware, as opposed to the earlier, expensive software encryption techniques.

This section has discussed the main objectives of database management systems. The next section reviews the two types of DBMSs that were originally developed to meet the needs of two distinct types of users.

2–2. Development of Database Management Systems

DBMSs can be classified in many ways.[1] For instance, most early DBMSs can be classified according to the type of user for whom they were designed. Although this classification has more historic than current importance, it should be discussed because some of the problems that arose because of this classification still plague DBMS developers and users.

In the late 1960s a data management problem arose, first within the intelligence community, but soon within many other types of organizations as well. End users—that is, nonprogramming users—needed to be able to ask a variety of unanticipated or ad hoc questions of their database and to receive a relatively fast response. ''Relatively fast'' in these cases meant seconds or minutes, as opposed to the days, weeks, or months it would have taken for a program to be written for each of these unanticipated queries. To meet this need, a variety of ''self-contained'' DBMSs were developed.

The data stored in the database were defined to the DBMS. More important, these DBMSs had a relatively simple query/update language for the end user. (Remember that the alternative to these early DBMSs were simple file systems, not other database management systems.) The query/update language was quick and easy to learn and allowed the end user to answer most of his questions himself, without the need for a specific program. These systems were called *self-contained database management systems.* Certain types of data could be put up on this type of database and essentially removed from the day-to-day concern of the data processing department. These early self-contained DBMSs were designed solely for the end user and therefore had no programming language interface for the programmer. While these self-contained systems were evolving, another completely different type of DBMS was also evolving in a different data processing environment.

As application systems and their data requirements became more complex, analysts and programmers were forced to spend more time and effort on routine data management functions, rather than on applications. A second type of DBMS evolved to meet this need: the *hosted DBMS*. Again, the data structure was defined and a set of data management routines was developed to do most of the routine data management operations for the programmer. The data manipulation language for these systems was not self-contained but was embedded or "hosted" within one or more programming languages. Information Management System (IMS) and its successors evolved to solve this type of problem— data management within the traditional data processing environment. The CODASYL Data Base Task Group report in 1971 was an attempt to identify the required database management functions and to provide a common COBOL interface for these hosted systems.[2] CODASYL systems are based on a network data structure and require the user, a programmer, to navigate through this compex data structure.

Although they were very different, both the self-contained and the hosted DBMSs provided some significant benefits and improvements in productivity. A number of different systems of both types evolved. A problem soon developed, however, because these two types of users and their databases were completely isolated from each other. If an end user needed a report or a query that included data from the hosted system, there was an impasse. Since the self-contained DBMSs had no programming language interface, it was impossible to access hosted databases from them. On the other hand, the programmer sometimes needed to use some of the data in the end user's self-contained database, but without a programming language interface this too was impossible. Finally, in some organizations with both a hosted and a self-contained DBMS, a more complex problem could occur. Either a programmer or an end user could have an application or a report that required combining data from both databases. One way to resolve this problem was to duplicate the data in both databases. This approach, though effective in the short run, was obviously unacceptable as a long-term solution. Therefore, the two types of DBMSs began to emerge. A programming language interface was added to the self-contained systems, and an end-user or high-level query language was added to the hosted systems. This development allowed either type of user—the programmer or the nonprogrammer end user—to access either database. This approach has become so accepted today that one no longer sees hosted or self-contained DBMSs. Almost all DBMSs now have this combined or complete capability.

Unfortunately, however, this dichotomy still affects some DBMS designers and implementers. There are still record-at-a-time, low-level data manipulation languages that force the programmer to navigate through the data structure, even in systems in which the end user is allowed to access the same database through a high-level query language. In principle, there is no reason that the high-level query language cannot also be embedded within the programming languages to provide this type of facility for the programmer.

2–3. Components of a Database Management System

This section describes the components and operation of database management systems in general. It provides a background for the 2–4 and 2–5 sections, which discuss CODASYL and relational database management systems, respectively, in more detail.

A database management system has four basic components: the database, the database definition, the data manipulation and query language, and the various data management procedures (that is, the actual DBMS software). Each of these four components is described in more detail in this section.

Database

The first component of the database management system is the database itself. These are the data that describe the various entities, attributes, and relationships of interest. An *entity type* refers to a specific kind of object, such as customers or orders. An *entity instance* or occurrence refers to a specific object of that type, such as customer number 12345. *Attributes* are characteristics of these entities. Each type of entity has a specific set of characteristics or attributes. A customer, for example, has a number, a name, an address, and a credit rating. All these attributes describe a customer, but some of them (the identification number) are identifiers that uniquely specify a particular customer. Most entity types have only one identifier, but it may be made up of several attributes. *Relationships* indicate the ways in which various entity types are linked. For example, a customer is related to his or her orders, and each order is related to a set of line items or parts that are being ordered.

All databases and their DBMSs are based on a specific data structure, which provides one way of classifying databases. Some databases consist of a set of flat files, that is, files with no repeating groups. This is the data structure used by most of the early file systems and is also the basic data structure for relational database systems. Other DBMSs assume a hierarchical data structure, wherein a node in the structure can have many children but only one parent. Still other DBMSs allow a network structure, wherein a node can have many parents as well as many children. Figure 2–1 summarizes these types of data structures. The two main types of DBMSs—the CODASYL and the relational—are discussed in sections 2–4 and 2–5. The aforementioned concepts (such as entity, attribute, and relationship) exist in both types of DBMSs and refer to aspects of the real world. Each type of DBMS has its own vocabulary

Hierarchy

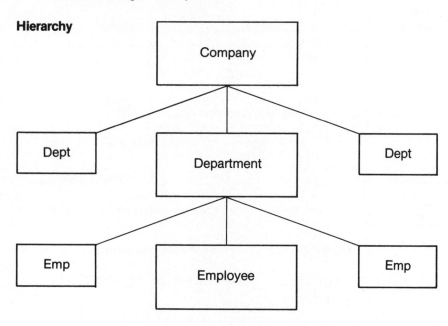

Network

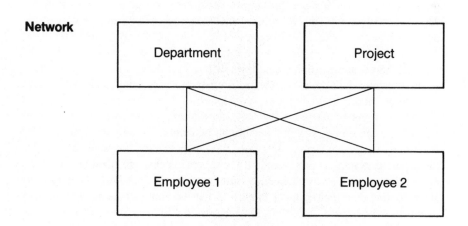

Figure 2–1. Data Structures

Real World	CODASYL	Relational
Entity Type	Record Type	Relation
Specific Entity	Record Occurrence	Tuple
Attribute	Data Item	Domain
Relationship	Set	Common Domain
Implementation of Relationship	Static, with Pointers	Dynamic, Join Operation

Figure 2–2. CODASYL-Relational Comparison

for representing these concepts within the database. Figure 2–2 summarizes these vocabulary differences.

Database Definition

The second component of a DBMS is the database definition, which may involve one, two, or three levels. Most DBMSs today have a two-level architecture for their database definition. These two levels are called the schema and the subschema. The *schema* provides a complete description of the entire database as it is stored. This definition includes the physical characteristics of the data, such as the format, the storage location, and the access paths to the data. The schema also defines the logical structure of the database. The definitions for CODASYL and relational databases differ. Therefore, a detailed discussion of the database definitions is deferred until sections 2–4 and 2–5, which concentrate on them.

The concept of levels of database definition is common to both types of DBMSs. In the single-level architecture the schema is the only level of database definition. Every application that uses the database uses the schema and sees the database exactly as it is stored. If the schema is changed, then normally the applications must also be changed. Single-level-architecture DBMSs do provide some routine data management functions, but the applications are very tightly bound to the database definition. Only by using a two- or three-level architecture is data independence, with all its benefits, possible.

In the two-level architecture the first-level definition is the schema, which is essentially the same as just described. The second level of data definition is provided by the subschema. The *subschema* describes that part of the database used by a particular application. It describes the database as the application expects it, rather than as it is actually stored. The subschema is similar to the schema except that it contains only logical characteristics of the database. Since the user should be completely isolated from the physical aspects of the database, the subschema does not need to define any of these characteristics. The subschema defines the entity types, their relationships, their attributes, and the format in which the application expects the data. The DBMS uses the schema and the subschema to map and convert the data between their stored form and the form expected by the application. The ability of the DBMS to do this mapping is what provides data independence.

The three-level architecture provides even greater data independence by further subdividing the schema into a logical and a physical part. The subschema is unchanged. Using the terminology of the three-level architecture, the overall logical data definition for the entire database is called the *conceptual schema*. It includes the logical definition that is now in the schema. The part of the schema that now provides the physical data definition is removed and placed in another level called the *internal schema*. The internal schema isolates all the physical and device-dependent characteristics of the database. For example, changes in the storage devices or the access mechanisms for performance improvement would require only changes in the internal schema. Changes in the logical access paths—that is, new relationships among record types—would, however, require changes in the conceptual schema as well as in the internal schema. The subschema, now called the *external schema,* is essentially unchanged. It describes the database as a particular application expects to see it. As with the two-level architecture, various DBMS procedures provide for the conversion and mapping of the data between the levels. Currently there are no commercially available DBMSs that uses this three-level architecture, but it has been proposed by the CODASYL Data Definition Language Committee.

Data Manipulation Language

The third component of a DBMS is the data manipulation or query language. Since the language is dependent on the data structure, it is discussed in more detail in the two sections on specific types of DBMSs. For either type of DBMS, however, the data manipulation language must allow the user to do four basic operations:

1. Retrieve data from the database.
2. Modify data already in the database.

3. Add new data to the database.
4. Delete data already in the database.

A data manipulation language can be at either a high or a low level. With a high-level language the user needs to specify only the data required, not how to obtain it, whereas with a low-level language the user must specify not only what data is required, but also the step-by-step procedure for obtaining it.

There are two common misunderstandings about data manipulation languages. The first is that the distinction between high and low levels relates to the type of DBMS that is used. The assumption is that CODASYL DBMSs require a low-level procedural language to navigate through the network, whereas relational DBMSs use high-level nonprocedural languages. Most, if not all, current CODASYL-based DBMSs provide both a high- and a low-level language. In these cases, a DBMS procedure converts the high-level query into a series of low-level procedural requests to do the necessary navigation.

The second misunderstanding is that the high-level query language is for the end user and the low-level language for the programmer. This is an artificial distinction. The programming user would get the same benefits from a high-level language that the end user does. This misunderstanding probably arises from the earlier distinction between self-contained and hosted DBMSs.

Database Procedures

The fourth component is the DBMS software: the procedures that actually perform the various database management functions. Examples of these procedures include determining whether a user has authorization to access the data, physically locating the data in the database, and doing the mapping between the schema and the subschema.

With some DBMSs the term *database procedure* is used in a narrower sense. Most DBMSs can be tailored to a limited extent. At certain points, the database administrator can insert his or her own local code to do certain special functions such as additional security checking. These local routines are what some systems narrowly refer to as database procedures.

The objectives and components of a database management system have been reviewed in this section. Sections 2–4 and 2–5 describe the specific operations of CODASYL and relational DBMSs. Section 2–6 discusses the similarity between the CODASYL and relational models and describes a common data model that allows different users to view the same database as either CODASYL or relational. This common data model permits the simplification of much of the later discussion on data distribution.

2–4. CODASYL Database Management Systems

This section discusses the architecture, organization, and operation of a CO-DASYL database management system. Although there are many DBMSs of this type, the purpose of this section is not to explain or describe any specific system but, rather, to provide an overview and an introduction to CODASYL-type DBMSs in general.

A database and a database management system are used to help an organization organize and control its data. There are various types of entities about which the organization needs to collect data. Within a CODASYL database, data about a specific type of entity is stored in a particular record type, usually named after the type of entity, for example, customer records, order records, employee records, or department records. The fields within in the record correspond to certain attributes or characteristics of the entity type. For example, customers have names, addresses, credit ratings, and credit limits. Most of these fields simply describe the entity, but a few of them (usually one per record type) are identifiers that uniquely specify a particular entity, for example, customer identification number or part number. In discussing a CODASYL database, one may refer to record types in general or to specific instances or occurrences of a record type. The record for customer 1234 is a specific instance or occurrence of a customer record.

Many of the entity types with which an organization must deal are related. For example, customers provide orders consisting of line items for parts in the inventory. Within the database, these entity relationships are represented by corresponding relationships among record types and among specific instances of these record types. For example, it must be possible to relate a particular instance of a customer record to all the order records for that customer. This relationship is provided by the concept of a *set*. The name given to the set describes the relationship, such as customer-order. When a set type is defined in the database schema, an owner record type and one or more member record types must be specified. For example, for the customer-order set, the owner record type is *customer* and the member record type is *order*. Set occurrences relate the occurrences of specific owner and member records. A specific instance of an order record can be a member of only one customer-order set. However, the order record may be either an owner or a member of other set types.

The rest of this section describes the data that are required to define a CODASYL database and the operations on the database. In the example that is discussed, there are only three record types: department, employee, and project. The structure of this database is shown in figure 2–3. There are several constraints on the database. People work in departments. Every employee must be a member of one and only one department. Employees may be assigned to

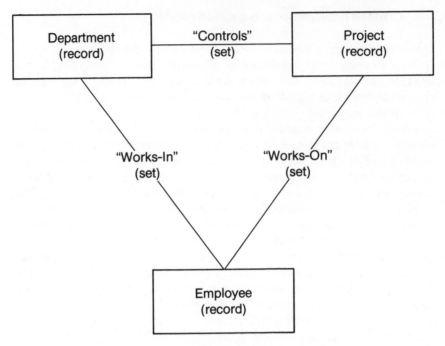

Figure 2–3. Example of CODASYL Structure

specific projects; however, it is possible that an employee is not assigned to a project. Finally, although departments are responsible for projects, people in other departments may also be assigned to a given project. In discussing the operation of the DBMS, four simple transactions are described.

1. List all the employees in the production department.
2. List all the employees on project X.
3. What is the total salary of the employees on project X?
4. Add an employee to the engineering department.

The definition of a CODASYL database has two parts, although they are not clearly differentiated. One part of the database definition relates to the logical structure of the data and the other part to the physical structure, that is, how the database is actually implemented. In current CODASYL systems, these logical and physical characteristics are combined into a single database definition.

The database administrator (DBA) must work with the various users of the database to determine their requirements and how they will use the database. Once he has done this, there are four elements that he must define: areas, records, fields, and sets. *Area* is a term used to designate both the storage plan of a database and the physical implementation of that plan. The storage plan for the database is contained in the area section of the database definition. The *record* section specifies each of the record types of which the database is composed. Each record definition also describes each *field* in the record. The final element that must be defined is the *set*. Every relationship between two or more record types must be defined in the set section. Each of these sections is described in more detail later.

First, each area of the database must be defined. Most of the area definition focuses on physical characteristics that affect the performance of the DBMS. First, the size of the area is defined in one of several ways. The simplest way is to specify a fixed size of N pages, where page size can also be arbitrarily defined. However, for more flexibility and more efficient use of storage, the definition should specify an initial size and allow the area to be expanded as needed up to a certain limit. Another option is to specify overflow pages in addition to the normal area. These overflow pages all may be grouped at the end of the area or may be scattered throughout the area with N overflow pages allocated for every M regular pages. In addition to the size specification, an initial load factor can also be specified. The initial load factor determines how much of a page is used when the database is initially loaded. If the area is volatile and is going to have many records added later, then specifying a low load factor forces the DBMS to leave room for additional records. By allowing the new records to be clustered physically near certain old ones on the same page, this method improves the performance of the database if both new and old records are frequently needed together. When the database is being loaded and the load factor for a page is reached, additional records that normally would be loaded onto that page are loaded onto the next page instead. This maintains the required amount of free space on the page for the later addition of new records.

The area definition also includes a recovery clause specifying the recovery procedure that will be used for the area. Depending on the volatility and importance of the data to be stored in an area, different backup and recovery procedures can be used for different areas. Possible alternatives usually include before images, after images, or both; but in those cases where the data is not critical, none of these procedures may be specified.

Second, each type of record in the database must be defined. The database contains data about various types of entities, and for each entity type there is usually a corresponding record type. A definition of each record type is included in the record section. The definition of each record type specifies the area or areas in which the records of that type must be stored. This specification is a physical database design decision and is made for performance reasons. The number of sets to which a record type may belong also affects its definition. The DBMS reserves pointer space in the record for the appropriate number of automatic sets, but the DBA must know and explicitly reserve the pointer space for the maximum number of manual sets to which a record of this type may belong. (The difference between manual and automatic sets is explained later when the set definition is described.)

The location mode of each record type must also be specified. This tells the DBMS how the records of each type are stored and retrieved. The three options are DIRECT, CALC, and VIA. With the DIRECT location mode the user specifies the specific area and page where each record is to be stored. Obviously, this approach completely violates all concepts of data independence and therefore should be avoided. It also requires that the user have detailed knowledge of how the database is structured and stored.

The CALC (calculation) location mode involves hashing. A key in the record is hashed into an area and page address that specifies where the record is to be stored. As part of the record definition, the DBA must specify the CALC key field or set of fields, the area in which the records of each type can be stored, and, as an option, the hashing algorithm. Allowing the DBA to specify the hashing algorithm for each record type permits more tuning of the database performance. With the CALC procedure, the DBMS automatically handles synonyms. The record definition also specifies whether or not duplicate keys are allowed. If the CALC key is the record identifier, then duplicates are not allowed and the DBMS will automatically make this check before it enters any new records. If the CALC key does not uniquely identify a record, then duplicates must be allowed. This option allows CALC records to be clustered on any set of fields. Clustering records this way can reduce the number of I/Os that are necessary to get a set of related records. This clustering is also part of the physical database design.

The third possible location mode for a record type is VIA. With this mode, a record instance is stored or retrieved by going through its owner record in a particular set. The VIA clause must also specify the set type to be used. This approach is appropriate when a record is normally used not by itself, but only within the context of its membership in a specific type of set. When VIA is used as the location mode, it is possible to specify the way the records are clustered so that member records are stored near their owner records in the set. Obviously, if a record type is a member of several set types, it can only be placed near one of the owner record types. The choice of owner type near which to locate it is based on the frequency with which each set is used. It should be placed near its owner in the set type in which it is used most frequently. This "place near" option is a physical performance characteristic and should be transparent to the user. It is simply part of the database performance tuning.

Third, each field within each record type must be defined. Since CODASYL originally concentrated exclusively on a COBOL interface, the field definition corresponds closely to the COBOL data-item definition. The basic definition for each field includes a level number, a name, a picture clause specifying the size and type of data to be stored in the field, and a usage clause.

If the field can be repeated, then an occurs clause is also needed. As with COBOL, the occurs clause can take one of two forms. The field can occur either a fixed number of times or a variable number of times. If it occurs a fixed number of times, then that number is given. If it can occur a variable number of times, then the range is given for the minimum and maximum number of occurrences, and another variable is specified on which the number of occurrences depends.

Fourth, the set types in the database must be defined. Relationships exist among various entity types in the real world. Within the database these relationships are represented by corresponding set types. Each of these set types must be defined so that the DBMS can maintain them. Part of the set definition relates to the logical structure of the set, but another part of it is related to the physical implementation of the set. The logical definition includes the set name, the owner record type, and the member record type or types. Each set type can have only one owner record type, but it can have several member record types.

The set mode must also be specified. This involves the way the set is actually implemented and how the members of the set are linked together. If, for example, there is a set type that links each customer record to all of its order records, then there must be a way for the DBMS to move from one order to the next for a specific customer. This mechanism is defined in the set-mode clause. The two options are chained and pointed array. In the former case, the member records are linked using a pointer chain. Each member-record occurrence (for example, order) has a pointer to the next member-record occurrence in the set. The last member of the set has a null pointer to indicate the end of the chain. If chaining is used, there may also be a prior pointer to the previous member record. This provides a two-way chain so that the DBMS can easily move forward or backward among the members of the set. These prior pointers are particularly important if the set is very volatile because they make it much easier to add or delete members. If the chained set mode is specified, then the types of pointers desired must also be specified.

The other mode for implementing a set is with a pointer array. This approach uses an inversion method. For each owner-record occurrence there is a list of pointers for the member records for that set occurrence. When a new member is added to a set occurrence, a new pointer is added to the pointer array for that owner record. Similarly, when a member is deleted from the set, the corresponding pointer in the array is deleted. The set mode concerns the physical implementation of the database and therefore should be completely transparent to the user. The mode for a set type is selected based on the frequency of various operations on that set type and the corresponding performance for each mode.

The set definition must also specify the position at which new member records are added to the set. The alternatives are FIRST, LAST, NEXT, PRIOR, and SORTED. FIRST, LAST, and SORTED specify an absolute position at which to add the new record, whereas NEXT and PRIOR specify relative positions. If most of the set activity involves its newest members, then they should be inserted at the beginning of the set's chain or pointer array to allow them to be found quickly without processing the entire set. This is done using the FIRST option. This approach might be used in an order processing system. In the opposite case, LAST specifies that the new members should be added at the end of the set. In still other cases the new member should be added in the appropriate position to maintain the proper sort sequence based on a key specified in the set definition. If duplicate key values are allowed, then the definition must also specify whether the new record should be added before or after the other set members with the same key value. The remaining two options, NEXT and PRIOR, specify a relative position at which to add a new set member. When a user is processing a CODASYL set, there is a pointer to the record in the set that he is currently using. NEXT and PRIOR indicate that the new record should be inserted either immediately after or just before this current record.

Finally, a set may be either automatic or manual. With an automatic set, every occurrence of a member record type must be a member of one of the set occurrences. For example, every employee must be assigned to a department. With a manual set, an occurrence of a member record type may or may not be a part of a set occurrence. For example, employees may or may not be assigned to projects. If a set is defined to be a manual one, then the user or the application program must explicitly link each record occurrence to the set, whereas with automatic sets the DBMS does this linkage automatically for the user.

So far this section has explained the concepts underlying a CODASYL DBMS and discussed what must be specified in its database definition. The rest of this section gives an example of the operation of a CODASYL DBMS for several sample transactions. Section 2–5 provides this same type of explanation and discussion for a relational type of DBMS. Section 2–6 shows the relationship between a CODASYL and a relational database and describes how to convert from a CODASYL to a relational database. This conversion is important because most of the research on distributed databases has focused on relational rather than CODASYL databases.

The rest of this section describes the way in which a CODASYL DBMS would process the four requests listed earlier.

1. *List all the employees in the production department.* The user of a CODASYL DBMS must navigate through the data structure. This means he must first find the proper department record and then find the employee records that are members of the WORKS-FOR set. Depending on how the department record type was defined, the user can use different methods to access it. For example, if the CALC mode were used, the user could access the record for the production department directly simply by specifying its key (the department code). In other situations the user might have to read each department record

in sequence and check its code to find the proper department. Once the user has the proper department record, he then requests the first member of that WORKS-FOR set occurrence. This provides him with the record for the first employee in the production department. Then, by using a series of GET NEXT commands, the user obtains the record for each of the employees in the department. An end-of-set indication is returned when all the employee records in the set have been processed. In an extreme case, a separate I/O may be required to obtain the department record and each employee record. If this type of request is made frequently, however, the employee records may be stored near their department record. In that case a single I/O would obtain many of the desired records. Many of the GET NEXT commands would then be able to get the next record from a buffer, rather than requiring another physical I/O.

2. *List all the employees in project X.* This request would be processed in the same way as the previous one, except that a different set type would be used. Depending on the relative frequencies of these two types of requests, the employee records could be clustered near either the department or the project record that was the owner of their set.

3. *What is the total salary of all employees on project X?* This request is similar to the previous one. The only difference is that instead of a listing of each employee record, this request requires that the salaries be summed as each employee record is obtained. In a CODASYL application program the programmer would have to navigate explicitly through this structure and examine each record to build up the sum. With a high-level query language, this request would be a single statement. The previous two requests could also be done with a single statement in a high-level query language. In these cases the DBMS rather than the user would decide how to navigate through the data structure.

4. *Add an employee to the engineering department.* As with the first request, the programmer would first have to find the proper department. Once the engineering-department record is found, the employee record must be inserted in the proper place. The proper position and its determination depend on how the set was defined. The set may be ordered on employee number. Alternatively, the set could have been defined so that new members would be inserted first or last. In any of these three cases the DBMS would automatically determine where to place the new record and would insert it in the proper position in the set. With the other two alternatives (NEXT and PRIOR) the user must determine where to place the new record. He does this by locating one of the current employee records. The new record is then placed immediately before (PRIOR) or after (NEXT) it. When the record is inserted, the DBMS automatically adds it to all the automatic sets of which it is a member. The user must explicitly specify when the record should be added to any manual sets of which it is a member.

This section has provided a brief introduction to CODASYL database management systems. The next section provides a comparable introduction for relational database management systems.

2–5. Relational Database Management Systems

This section provides a basic introduction to relational database management systems. In 1970 Codd proposed a relational data model as an alternative to the network and hierarchical models.[3] In the past ten years the relational model has become widely accepted in both research and development and academic circles. However, there has been much less acceptance in the commercial environment. This lack of acceptance is partly due to the new concepts and terminology involved and partly to the fact that until very recently there were no commercially available relational DBMSs. Relational systems were available primarily in research and development and university environments, and their performance left much to be desired. This is now beginning to change with the advent of several commercially available systems, such as ORACLE from RSI and the IDM-500 from Britton-Lee. Nevertheless, there is still no widely accepted relational system or "standard" comparable to the CODASYL approach. Also, there are not yet any very large (10-billion byte) relational databases. However, because of the growing importance of relational systems, especially in the distributed database area, this section provides an introduction to them. It first discusses the basic concepts, then the data definition, and finally the operation of a hypothetical relational DBMS using the same sample transactions that were used in the CODASYL section. Section 2–6 shows the relationship between CODASYL and relational DBMSs and describes how to convert from a CODASYL to a relational database.

There is a basic problem in defining a relational DBMS. Obviously, it is one that uses a relational data model, but at what level? If a relational query language is placed on top of an underlying CODASYL DBMS, does it become a relational DBMS? Regardless of the query language, must the underlying DBMS implementation be relational for the system to qualify as a relational one? How many relational features must a DBMS have before it qualifies as a relational system? At present there are no clear answers to these questions. For the purposes of this book, however, the DBMS must at least appear relational to the user; that is, it must at least have a relational query language. Today, few if any relational systems, except some of those implemented on special-purpose database computers, really have an underlying relational implementation. The reader should realize that this definitional problem exists but should focus on the characteristics of the DBMS rather than its label.

As with a CODASYL database, a relational database is used to describe various types of entities, their characteristics, and the relationships among them. The vocabulary is different, however. The data about a certain type of entity are stored in a relation or a table. The database consists of one or more different types of relations. For example, there might be department, employee, and project relations. The entry for a specific entry (employee 1234) is called a *tuple*. The order in which these tuples are stored in a relation is irrelevant. The individual characteristics of an entity are described in the domains (fields) within the relation. Thus the employee relation would have domains for the employee number, name, address, salary, department, and any other attributes of interest. Most of the domains in a relation simply describe a characteristic of the entity, but one domain (or a set of concatenated domains) called the *key* can be used to identify the tuple for a specific entity uniquely.

Normalization, one of the steps in designing a relational database, involves the degree to which the domains in a relation are dependent on the key domain. If a relation has no repeating groups, it is in first normal form. The relation is in second normal form if, in addition, all the other domains in the relation are functionally dependent on the key. If the further restriction is added that the domains must be functionally dependent only on the key (that is, all the other domains are mutually independent), then the relation is the third normal form. Relational databases are designed in part by clustering the domains in such a way that the relations are in third normal form. Using this form simplifies updating because it avoids certain types of updating problems, such as a ripple effect whereby changing a domain in a tuple of one relation forces a domain to be changed in many other tuples in other relations. Normalization is one way to solve this type of updating problem. Another alternative is to define the database so that the DBMS can determine whether there will be a ripple effect and, if so, let it make the additional changes automatically.

Relationships among different types of entities are represented by relationships among different types of relations. In a CODASYL database these relationships are implemented by sets that must be specified when the database is defined. These set relationships are then implemented by pointers and indexes of various kinds. In a relational database these relationships are implemented by having a common domain in both relations. For example, tuples in the employee relation are linked to appropriate department tuples because the department number is in both relations. Any two relations can be linked by any domains they have in common. This ability to link a pair of relations dynamically is what provides relational DBMSs with greater flexibility than CODASYL systems. Unfortunately, the performance penalty incurred to provide this flexibility is one of the major handicaps of relational systems.

So far this section has described the basic concepts underlying the relational model. The rest of the section discusses the definition of a relational database and the basic operations of a relational DBMS.

There are some similiarities between the definitions of a relational and a CODASYL database. In both cases there is a logical and a physical component to the definition. At the logical level, each relation in the database must be defined. There must also be a complete definition of each domain in each relation. This part of the definition is equivalent to the record and item definitions in CODASYL. Various constraints on relations and domains may also be included in this logical definition.

Because there are many ways in which relational systems can be implemented, there is relatively little commonality in their physical definition. For example, some relational database definitions may not have the equivalent of a set definition because they are able to create these relationships dynamically. For performance reasons, however, some relational DBMSs may allow the DBA to define frequently used connections, such as the department number as the common domain joining the department and the employee relations. These connections may then be implemented by pointers and indexes. In the relational system this would be part of the physical rather than the logical definition because it involves the way the database is implemented rather than the way the user sees it. Any other connections the user requested could still be done dynamically, so the user would still see this relational capability.

A relational database definition may also include the concept of physical areas. If it did, then its area definition could be very similar to the CODASYL definition. It would specify the size of the area, the relations that would be stored in the area, and the recovery procedures to be used for that area. Again, this part of the definition involves the physical implementation of the database and should be completely transparent to the user. Everything that was said about the area definition in the CODASYL discussion would also apply to the area definition in a relational system.

A relational DBMS has three basic operations—selection, projection, and join. The *selection* operation identifies the set of tuples to be processed. This is done with a boolean selection expression. For example, the query, "list all the engineers in the production department," would have a selection expression specifying that job code equals engineer and department code equals production. The selection operation would search the employee relation to identify all the tuples that met these criteria. Depending on the sophistication of the DBMS, the user may or may not have to specify the relations to use.

The second operation is *projection*. Each relation has many domains, but in most cases the user is interested in only a few of them. Projection allows the user to specify which domains should be processed. For example, a request may ask for a list of the name, address, and department for all the engineers in the company. This involves a combination of selection (job code equals engineer) and projection (list only name, address, and department). Both selection and projection always involve a single relation type and result in reducing the amount of data to be processed.

The third operation, the *join*, involves multiple relation types and increases the amount of data. The join is used when a request requires data from two or more relations. The join operation combines the appropriate tuples in two relations. (If more than two relations are involved, the join is repeated until all the necessary data have been combined.) For example, if a request needed employee, department, and project data, the employee and department relations would be joined. Then the resulting relation would be joined with the project relation. In many cases, all three operations are used together in a single request.

The previous section described the operation of a CODASYL DBMS in processing four typical transactions. The rest of this section uses these same four transactions to describe the operation of a relational system. However, this description is primarily at a logical rather than a physical level because of the variations in how relational systems may be implemented. The four transactions are:

1. List all the employees in the production department.
2. List all the employees on project X.
3. What is the total salary of all employees on project X?
4. Add an employee to the engineering department.

The database contains three relations—employees, departments, and projects. Department number is the common domain linking employees and departments. Projects can be linked to either employees or departments. Assume that the common domains providing these links are E-proj and D-proj.

1. List all the employees in the production department. This transaction requires a simple selection of those employee tuples where the department code equals production. A projection also could have been used with this transaction. If this had been done, then only the specified domains would have been listed. To process this request, the relational DBMS would simply scan the entire employee relation and select those in the production department. Some relational systems might provide an option so that if the DBA knew that this was going to be a frequent type of request, a set of indexes could be built up for department code. This would allow the search to be done much more quickly than by actually scanning the entire relation each time.

2. List all the employees on project X. For a relational system, this request is identical to the previous one except that the section expression involves a different domain. Again, depending on the way the relational DBMS was implemented, this request could be processed by scanning the employee or by using a predefined index.

A complication would arise only if an employee could be assigned to several projects. If this were the case, there would have to be an intermediate or linking relation that would contain only the employee number and the project number. This intermediate relation would be required because a relation cannot have repeating groups (for example, a single employee relation cannot have multiple project numbers). If the intermediate relation were required, then processing the transaction would be more complicated. The first step would be to do a selection on the intermediate relation to obtain those tuples for project X. Then the selected tuples would be joined with the employee relation. This would then provide a list of all of the requested employees. The user who asked for the list of employees would not need to know which approach was used.

3. What is the total salary of all employees on project X? This high-level transaction is a simple extension of the foregoing request. In the previous case the list of employees was provided to the user. In this case the DBMS would process the list to sum up the salaries and then return the total to the user.

4. Add an employee to the engineering department. This transaction involves adding another tuple to the employee relation. Depending on the database definition, various validity checks may be performed. Various domains within the relation can be checked for validity. Since the employee must be assigned to an existing department, a check can be made to ensure that the department relation does have a tuple for the engineering department. If the employee had to be assigned to a project, a similar check could be made with the project relation.

There are two key differences that distinguish the add in the relational DBMS from the add in the CODASYL DBMS. First, when the employee tuple is added, the links do not have to be explicitly established linking it to the appropriate tuples in other relations. This linkage will be made dynamically whenever necessary. Second, the position of the employee tuple in the employee relation is irrelevant, whereas in a CODASYL DBMS this ordering may be important.

Throughout this section on relational systems, there have been a number of comparisons with the CODASYL approach. The next section makes the relationship between the two types of sytems even more explicit by describing how to convert from a CODASYL database to an equivalent relational database. This conversion capability is important because most of the databases that exist today are based on the CODASYL or network data model, but most of the work being done in the distributed database management area is predicated on the relational data model.

2–6. CODASYL to Relational Database Conversion

This section describes a basic procedure for converting from a CODASYL database to the equivalent relational database. This conversion capability will be required to allow many users to convert their current CODASYL or network databases to the relational systems on which much of the distributed database management work is predicated. Because of the many variations in the way relational systems can be implemented, most of this discussion focuses on conversion at the logical rather than the physical level. Once the logical structure of a CODASYL database has been converted to the logical structure of a relational database, the actual physical implementation of that relational structure should be relatively easy.

The key to the conversion problem is to find a way to map two CODASYL structures into the equivalent relational structures. This must be done in such a way that the relational DBMS can process relational transactions against the database. The complication is that it must also be possible for the unconverted programs that used the CODASYL database to continue to process it as if there had been no change. The two key differences between the CODASYL and relational approaches involve the static versus the dynamic definition and construction of relationships, and the importance of position. Each of these two differences is considered later.

In a CODASYL, database sets are used to statically define the relationships between entities. These linkages are established when the database is defined. A relational system allows these linkages to be made dynamically. Therefore, when the conversion is made, enough information must be included in the new relations to allow the relational mechanisms to be used to reconstruct the CODASYL sets when they are needed. This can be done simply by pushing down the key of every set owner into all of the members of the set. For example, the key of a department record is pushed down into the employee record from each employee in the department. Now, by examining an employee record, the relational DBMS can link it to the appropriate owner or department record.

In principle, these keys can be pushed down through any number of levels. The division code can be pushed down into the department. Either the department code alone or both the division and the department codes can then be pushed down into the employee record. One approach is to make an arbitrary decision to push all keys down either one level or through all levels of the data structure. The alternative is to allow the DBA the flexibility to specify how far down each key should be passed. The decision is based on a trade-off between storage and processing costs. Pushing a key down through more levels requires additional storage. The trade-off is that then some requests can be processed using a single relation rather than requiring a join. Even when a join is required, pushing a key down through several levels may reduce the number of joins that are required.

The keys must be pushed down in every set of which the record is a member. For example, an employee can be a member of two sets, one relating him to a department and one relating him to a project. Therefore, both department and project keys must be pushed down into the employee record. This allows the relational DBMS to reconstruct either set whenever necessary.

Pushing down keys does appear to increase the size of the database—but by how much? One study of a manufacturing system indicated that the increase was relatively modest. Initially, there was an expansion of 15 to 20 percent.

However, further analysis reduced this to about 5 percent. The reason for this reduction is that many CODASYL databases are designed in such a way that many keys are already pushed down. For example, order records frequently include the customer number, and employee records may already include the department number. In these cases additional storage is not required. The DBMS simply must be told which are the common fields in the two records. Another reason for the modest increase in size is that once the keys have been pushed down, the pointers that were previously used to indicate the set relationships are no longer necessary.

The other major difference between the CODASYL and relational approaches, involves the importance of position within the set. In CODASYL, position can be important, whereas in a relational system the position of a tuple is irrelevant. Therefore, if the CODASYL applications are to be able to continue to process the converted database, there must be a way to maintain the position of a record within a set. This can be done by using a sequence field for each set. Although the tuples in the relational format may not actually be stored in the CODASYL order, whenever a CODASYL user wants the set, it can be sorted and presented to him in the proper order. Each record must have a sequence number for every set of which it is a member. The way in which the sequence numbers are implemented depends on how records can be inserted in the set. The alternative insertion methods were described in the set-definition section of the CODASYL database discussion. If the set is sorted on a specific data item, then that item can serve as the sequence field. In the other cases a new sequence field must be added to the record. If the new records are inserted either FIRST or LAST, then the sequence numbers can be assigned arbitrarily by simply adding or subtracting one to or from the previous number. If the insertions are done either NEXT or PRIOR, then a space must be left between the numbers for future insertions. For example, sequence numbers could be assigned using an increment of ten. This would allow nine new records to be inserted between any two existing records. If a tenth record had to be added between them, then the set would have to be resequenced, but this is a very simple operation.

In summary, two simple mechanisms—pushing down keys and adding sequence fields for each set—allow a CODASYL database to be converted to an equivalent relation form. Obviously, the conversion between a specific CODASYL DBMS and a specific relational DBMS is more complex because of the ways in which they may be implemented. These two mechanisms, however, provide the key for the conversion routines.

2–7. Summary

This chapter has provided a basic introduction to database management systems. It began by discussing the objectives of database management and went on to identify the components of a DBMS and to explain their operations. Next, it described in some detail the most common type of DBMS, a CODASYL system. It then discussed the relational database management approach. It concluded by showing the similarity between the two types of DBMSs and explaining a basic procedure for converting from a CODASYL to a relational database.

The next chapter provides a basic introduction to the concepts of data communications.

Notes

1. J.P. Fry and E.H. Sibley, "Evolution of Data Base Management Systems," *Computing Surveys* 8, no. 1 (March 1976):7–42.

2. CODASYL Systems Committee, *Feature Analysis of Generalized Data Base Management Systems,* (New York: Association for Computing Machinery; 1971).

3. E.F. Codd, "A Relational Model of Data for Large Shared Data Banks," *Communications of the ACM* 13, no. 6 (June 1970):377–387.

3　Data Communications

Distributed database management systems are the results of the merging of data communications and database management. The purpose of this data communications chapter is to provide enough background so that those who are not data communications experts can understand and address the communications issues that arise in planning, designing, and developing distributed database management systems. The purpose is not to create data communications experts but simply to enable the reader to understand the communications problems that arise and to discuss them with the data communications experts who must actually solve them. Therefore, the purpose of chapter 3 is similar to that of chapter 2. Distributed database management requires a certain amount of expertise in both database management and data communications. Each of these chapters attempts to provide the necessary background in one area for experts in the other area. Therefore, data communications experts may review this chapter relatively quickly, but the reader should make sure that all the concepts are familiar. This chapter consists of sections dealing with basic concepts, communications technologies, communications architectures, and the open systems interconnection model, followed by a summary.

3–1. Basic Concepts

In a distributed system, there are two basic hardware components—nodes and communications paths.[1] A *node* is a processing element that contains both processing power and memory. Depending on the type of node, it may also include secondary storage. A node may be a large mainframe, a mincomputer, or a microcomputer. The software that runs in the node must include some communications functions to allow the node to communicate with the rest of the network. In larger nodes, such as mainframes, the communications software may coexist with application programs and other support software, including operating systems and database management systems. Some of the smaller nodes, however, may be dedicated to communications or message-switching functions, in which case they contain only communications software. These dedicated nodes are called front-end processors, cluster controllers, communications processors, or network-control processors. In some cases they include special hardware, but in many cases they are simply general purpose processors with special communications software. Section 3–4 discusses the functions this

33

software must perform and how the ISO has proposed to organize them into specific layers.

The other type of component in a distributed system is the communications paths or links that connect the nodes. Many characteristics are associated with communications, some of them associated with the communications lines and others really characteristics of the communications system as a whole. The two main characteristics of a communications path are its bandwidth and its mode.

Bandwidth is a hardware characteristic of a communications line. It refers to the amount of information or the number of bits that can be transmitted per second (bps). Bandwidths can be classified into several ranges:

1. subvoice (less than 200 bps)
2. voice (600 to 4,800 bps)
3. broadband (50,000 bps and up)

In some cases there is a significant difference between the speed of a terminal device and that of the line to which it is attached. In these cases, buffers are used to match the speeds. If the terminal is faster than the communications line, then its access capacity is unused, as when a CRT is used at teletype speeds because of a subvoice-grade line. On the other hand, if the line is much faster than the device, one can use its excess capacity by multiplexing many devices over the same communications line. Similarly, subvoice lines or channels can be multiplexed and transmitted simultaneously over the same voice-grade line. Voice-grade lines can be multiplexed over a single broadband line. Although broadband lines are considered to be 50,000 bps and up, there are some very high bandwidth technologies that permit millions of even billions of bits per second.

The second characteristic is the *mode* of a path. A path can be simplex, half duplex, or full duplex. A simplex path can transmit in only one direction. An example is the path from a remote sensor to a data-collection computer. In this case the data could be sent only from the sensor to the computer, not in the reverse direction. Simplex lines are relatively cheap, but they have no flexibility. The two duplex modes provide greater flexibility because they can be used in either direction. A full-duplex path can transmit in both directions simultaneously. A half-duplex path can transmit in either direction, but in only one direction at a time. However, a delay is incurred when the direction of the transmission changes with a half-duplex path. This turnaround time can create a significant delay if a node is sending many very short messages and getting an acknowledgement for each of them. Half-duplex lines are more effective with fewer, relatively long messages. Full-duplex lines, though more expensive, do not have this delay. Dial-up lines are usually half duplex, whereas leased lines are usually full duplex.

Bandwidth and mode are characteristics of only the communications line.

However, there are other performance characteristics that are more closely related to the overall system. They are the results of the way the entire communications system is structured. These characteristics include transfer rate, path-establishment time, network delay, and reliability.

The end user of the communications system is more interested in the transfer rate than in the bandwidth. They involve two different concepts. The bandwidth, which is determined by the communication path's technology, is simply the number of bits that can be transmitted over the line in a given period of time. However, to the end user many of these bits represent overhead, not useful information. A message includes certain header information as well as the actual message. The header specifies the source and destination of the message and uniquely identifies the message. The message itself also contains redundant information (such as parity) for error detection and correction. In many systems, however, when an error is detected, the message is retransmitted. This retransmission is also overhead since it provides no increase in useful information for the user. The bandwidth of the line must be used to transmit both the user's message and all the additional information required by the communications system. This means that the actual transfer rate for the user's messages may be significantly less than the bandwidth would seem to allow. This difference is significant when most of the messages are relatively short. Furthermore, if the messages are routed through intermediate nodes, then additional delays may be incurred by the communications software at each of these intermediate nodes. In summary, the transfer rate—that is, the rate at which the end user's messages are actually transferred between the source and destination nodes—is frequently less than the actual bandwidth of the path. Also because of various random factors involved in communications (such as error rates and delays in the communications software), the transfer rate is a statistical characteristic, rather than a precise number like bandwidth.

The path-establishment time is the time it takes for the communications system to select and activate a communications path once one has been requested. A logical path is established once when a session is created. The physical implementation of this logical path may be created at the same time, but in many cases it is created dynamically for each message or packet. With a dial-up line, the physical link is established when the session is created. In this case, the path-establishment time is the time it takes to dial the number and for the devices at both ends of the path to complete the necessary handshaking procedures and protocols to verify that the link has been established. This can involve a significant delay—as much as several seconds—which would be prohibitive if this process had to be repeated for each transaction. If the session lasts for minutes or hours, however, this overhead is insignificant. With packet switching and local networks, there is a permanent path linking the nodes. In these cases, path establishment simply involves selecting the link once the source and destination nodes are known. This procedure is much faster and can be done for each transaction without excessive performance penalties. In fact, a packet-switching system does this for each packet within a message. To select the type of link between two nodes, the system designer must analyze the communications patterns to determine how frequently the path would have to be established, the cost and delay incurred each time it is established, and how often a permanent channel would be idle. The key trade-offs involve the bandwidth, the response time, and the cost.

Network delay is a measure of how long it takes to send a message through the network from the sources to the destination node. There are two major causes for this delay. First, there is the propagation delay, that is, the time it takes for a signal to be transmitted from one node to another. Since the transmission is at the speed of light, this delay is usually negligible, except with satellite communications, in which case the delay, about one-fifth of a second, can be significant in terms of processing speeds. The second type of delay is in the communications software that must be executed in both the source and the destination nodes. Additional software delays occur at any intermediate nodes. For example, with a packet-switching system, these software delays involve disassembling the message into individual packets, routing each of them through the network (possibly over different paths), and finally reassembling the message at the destination node. The amount of delay caused by the communications software depends on the functions it provides for the user. As with database management systems, there is a trade-off between functionality and performance.

Another characteristic of a communcations systems is its reliability. A communications system is reliable if it can ensure that once it has accepted a message, the message will be delivered to its destination in an accurate and timely fashion. The concepts of availability and accuracy are closely related to reliability. A communications system or a specific path within the system is available if it will accept a message when the user wants to send one. If the link has failed or been disconnected for some reason, it is not available. At this point, the user knows the message has not been accepted and can try to transmit it again later. Reliability is only involved once the communications system has accepted the message. A reliable communications system ensures that once the message has been accepted, it will eventually be delivered, even if some parts of the communications system fail. The importance of this concept is shown in chapter 8, wherein all the update synchronization procedures discussed assume the existence of a reliable communications system that provides this guaranteed delivery.

A reliable communications system must also ensure that the message is delivered accurately. There are many techniques to detect and correct errors when they occur. In some cases error-correcting codes allow the receiving node to detect and correct a single error. Most of these systems also allow the detection (but not the correction) of two errors. In these cases, if two errors (or a single error, in non-error-correcting systems) occur, the receiving node may request that the message be repeated. In other cases the receiving node does not need to take any action. If the message is not acknowledged within a certain time period, it is automatically retransmitted. Either of these approaches provides enough time delay for most transient problems, such as a burst of static on the line, to disappear. If the problem remains after several attempts, then an alternate path must be used. Therefore, a communications system is much more reliable if it is able to reroute messages or packets dynamically when a particular communications path fails. In some cases, it may be temporarily impossible for two nodes to communicate—for example, when the only link between the two nodes is down. In this case, a reliable system would store the message until the link was reestablished and then transmit it. Various communications techniques, such as dynamic routing, error-detection and -correction codes, message and packet sequence numbers, and store and forward procedures make it possible for the overall system to be far more reliable than the components from which it is built.

The requirements of the various applications that use the communications network determine the complexity and sophistication of the system's reliability techniques. Communications systems used in real-time command and control or process control require much greater reliability than those used for a time-sharing system. Similarly, the message-processing system for an electronic mail application can be less reliable than one used by an electronic funds transfer system. The designer of the communications system must know and explain the various trade-offs that can be made. However, it is the user who must actually make the trade-off and decide which factors are the most important for his application.

3–2. Communications Technologies

The importance of communications technologies arises from the different cost-performance trade-offs provided by the various technologies. One of the driving forces behind distributed processing in general and distributed database management in particular is the cost-performance trade-offs between processing and communications. Different communications technologies can drastically alter this trade-off, however. The use of a communications system with voice-grade lines would result in a very different set of trade-offs and a different systems design than the use of a communications system based on fiber optics technology. This section provides a brief overview of the range of technologies that are currently available and the way they affect the trade-off.

There are three general levels of communications technology. The first level is *intracomputer communications,* which involves the movement of data among the various parts of a single computer. Its implementation depends on the specific computer system architecture. This type of communications frequently involves very high speed, bit-parallel, synchronous data paths between each pair of components in the computer system. The data unit that is transmitted in parallel consists of one or more bytes of data plus the associated control bits. Larger, faster systems transmit larger blocks of data in parallel. This type of communications path requires expensive computer cabling, which is usually limited to a few hundred feet. This provides a dedicated path between each pair of components. The other intracomputer communications approach involves a high-speed bit-serial bus which is shared by all of the components. Whenever a component has a message to send, it obtains control of the bus, sends its message, and releases the bus. The first part of the message contains the address of the node or component to which the message is being sent. Each node examines the destination address of each message and accepts any message directed to it. Both these types of intracomputer communications are really special cases and are not normally considered as part of distributed systems. Their bandwidths, response times, costs, and distance limitations are of different orders of magnitude from the more common types of communications used in most distributed systems. This may be changing, however, because some of the newer technologies, such as fiber optics, are now being proposed and used in some local networks. The integration of these newer communications technologies into local networks will force significant changes in the architectural assumptions underlying distributed systems design.

Evolving communications technology is creating local networks as a second, intermediate level of communications. *Local networks* represent a compromise between the cost-performance of intracomputer communications and that of the more traditional types of communications.[2] These networks are relatively limited geographically, usually between a few thousand feet and a few miles. They are usually owned and used by a single organization, such as a university, or a factory complex. From the organization's perspective there is a significant difference between local networks and the more traditional public communications systems. With the local network, the organization has much greater control over the system and how it is used. Functionally, these local networks are similar to the third traditional type of communications described below, but in terms of cost-performance they are closer to the intracomputer types of communications. Local networks are usually implemented with higher-performance, more expensive technology, which is still prohibitively expensive to use on a large scale. This technology does, however, allow a different set of design trade-offs than are possible with traditional communications.

A third type of communications system is what is normally considered with *distributed processing*. These are the relatively slow technologies used in the public communications systems provided by the common carriers. These systems are used in widely dispersed geographic networks that cover one or more countries. "Relatively slow" in this sense may be up to 50- or 100-kb broadband communications lines, but even these rates are slow compared with the internal processing speeds of current processors, or even with the communications technologies used to implement local networks. The relative cost-performance differences between these communications systems and processor technology determine many of the design trade-offs made in most current distributed systems. This is the type of communications technology used by most distributed database management systems, both now and in the immediate future. Further in the future, however, more emphasis will have to be placed on those technologies now being used in local networks, for two reasons. First, as the cost of these technologies is reduced, it will become feasible to use them in much more dispersed communications systems. Second, as local networks become more widely used, they will begin to include distributed database management capabilities.

3–3. Communications Architecture

A communications architecture provides a way of classifying communications systems and of organizing the various components within them. Although there are many ways to classify communications systems, Anderson and Jensen have proposed one of the better classifications.[3] The discussion in this section is organized around their architecture. In terms of their architecture, a communications system consists of three types of components—processing elements or nodes, communications paths, and switches. The communications paths link the various nodes within the system and are used to send messages between source and destination nodes. The characteristics of these paths have been described in a previous section. Routing decisions are made by switches within the system. These may be special purpose hardware switches or processing elements performing a switching function. The taxonomy of communications systems consists of a set of four decisions, as shown in figure 3–1. These decision levels are transfer strategy, control method, path structure, and system architecture. Each of these levels is discussed later.

The first design decision in the architecture involves the transfer strategy, which may be either direct or indirect. With the direct strategy, a message is sent directly between the source and destination nodes with no intermediate processing. The indirect transfer strategy involves some intermediate processing or routing. Any of this intermediate processing is done by switches.

The second decision level involves the control method that is used with the indirect strategy. With the direct transfer strategy, there is no intervening control method. If the transfer strategy is indirect, then at least one intermediate switch must perform some control or routing function. This control function may be either centralized or distributed. With centralized control, all the routing is done at a central switch. With distributed control, there are several nodes—

Decisions	**Alternatives**
1. Transfer Strategy	Direct, Indirect
2. Transfer Control Method	Centralized, Decentralized None
3. Transfer Path Structure	Dedicated, Shared
4. System Architecture (many specific implementations)	Loop, Star, Bus, Complete Interconnection

Figure 3–1. Anderson-Jensen Communications Taxonomy

possibly even all the nodes—that can make routing decisions. These nodes can make routing decisions essentially independently of each other. For a node to perform this control or routing function, it must have certain information. The main data elements required are the source- and destination-node identifiers and the routing matrix, which indicates which nodes are linked together and the characteristics of each path.

The third decision level involves the path structure. A path is either dedicated or shared. A *dedicated* path is used only for communications between two specific nodes. Stars and completely interconnected systems use dedicated paths. A *shared path* is a common path used by several nodes. Bus structures are the most common examples of shared paths. With shared paths, contention can arise over which node can have access to the path at a particular instant. The way in which this contention is resolved varies with different systems, but these methods are not relevant for the discussion at this point.

The fourth level determines the specific system architecture. This level of the design decision distinguishes between specific architectures that are similar on all the previous levels. For example, either shared memory or a global bus can be used to implement communications with a direct transfer strategy and shared paths. It is only at the system-architecture level that these two approaches are different.

A communications architecture has been defined when a decision has been made for each of these four levels. Anderson and Jensen then evaluate various architectures based on five criteria: modularity, connection flexibility, fault tolerance, bottlenecks, and logical complexity. Each criterion will be discussed.

Modularity refers to the ease with which the system can be expanded. Ideally, it should be easy to add nodes and expand the system. However, certain design decisions seriously affect this modularity. The two extreme examples of modularity are the *star* and the *completely interconnected system*. With a star communications topology, wherein all the nodes must communicate through a single central node (a central switch), the modularity is very high. To add another node, all that is needed, in addition to the node itself, is a single communications path to the central node and the modification of its routing table. This means that the modularity for adding another node is very high. On the other hand, the modularity for adding another central switch—for example, to improve the systems reliability—is very low. Not only must a central switch be added, but new communications paths also must be provided connecting the new switch to every node in the network. With the completely interconnected approach, modularity is very low because when a node is added, a new path must be provided from the new node to every other node in the system. Furthermore, the addition of another node in such a system tremendously increases the number of possible communications paths with which the routing algorithms must deal.

Connection flexibility concerns the number of ways in which a message can be routed between two nodes. The more possible paths there are, the greater the connection flexibility. This flexibility is not important in itself, although it can complicate the routing algorithms. The real importance of connection flexibility is its impact on the system's reliability. Greater connection flexibility means that there are more paths over which a message can be routed between nodes, which in turn means greater reliability if a particular path fails.

Fault tolerance involves the ability of the system to continue to operate after one or more failures have occurred. Either a node or a communications path can fail. Obviously, if a node fails, then any processing that was being done on that node either must be done at another node or must be delayed until the failed node has been repaired. However, from a communications perspective, the failure of either a node or a path should neither cause the system to fail nor even significantly delay the transmission of messages through the system. In some systems, especially those using the complete-interconnection approach, there are several paths between any given source and destination node pair. Therefore, the failure of any path or intermediate node should not result in the isolation of any other node, because there are always alternate paths that can be used. On the other hand, the failure of a path in a loop or ring architecture causes a catastrophic failure. A similar problem occurs with star architecture if the central switching node fails: all the nodes are then isolated. The star, however, is much more tolerant of a failure of a communictions path or of one of the noncentral nodes. These failures would not cause a catastrophic failure of the entire system. Even if one of the nodes becomes isolated, the rest of the system can continue to function.

The fourth criterion involves *system bottlenecks*. As the load on a system increases, different architectures bottleneck at different points. A star architecture can easily become overloaded and bottleneck at the central switch. Shared communications paths, such as busses, also can easily overload and greatly increase the response time for the system if the communications demand peaks simultaneously at several nodes. Depending on how the communications system is designed, different parts of it can create the bottleneck. However, most architectures have one element that is more likely to bottleneck than the others. Ideally, the system should be modular in terms of this component so that the bottleneck can be eliminated easily when it does occur.

The fifth criterion is *logical complexity*. It refers to the number and complexity of the decisions that must be made to allow and control communications between a source and destination node. The number and complexity of these decisions determine the complexity of the communications software required to support a given architecture. For example, a fully interconnected system requires a far more complex routing algorithm than does a simple loop structure. Further complexity is introduced into the software by the architecture's fault tolerance and recovery procedures. This is especially true when the failure causes the system to change its basic architecture. This could occur when one or more dedicated paths are lost and a system must begin to route messages through intermediate nodes, thus shifting from dedicated to shared paths.

This section has discussed communications architecture in general. It has provided a way of classifying different architectures and described a set of criteria for evaluating them. The next section focuses on a specific architecture—the *open systems interconnection model* being proposed by the International Standards Organization.

3–4. Open Systems Interconnection Reference Model

There has been much discussion about developing a standard communications architecture.[4] A standard architecture would provide three benefits. First, it would allow different networks and their components to communicate with each other. Second, a well-designed, layered architecture would simplify the design and development of communications systems. Finally, a standard architecture would protect the user's investment in his communications-oriented applications software. This section describes the open systems interconnection (OSI) architecture now being proposed by the ISO as the basis for future communications standards.

The use of terminals, multiple computer systems, and communications networks is becoming widespread. Initially, all the processing logic was in the central computer, with very simple terminals communicating with it on a character-by-character basis. This method was slow and created a tremendous overhead on the central computer. Now with the proliferation of fast, inexpensive microprocessors, more intelligence is being placed into the terminals so that part of the communications-related processing can be offloaded from the central computer. The proliferation of various terminals and devices creates a problem because currently communications requirements and formats are very different. Furthermore, this problem is becoming even more serious because communications is becoming an integral part of many, if not most, computer systems. Currently, many vendors have their own internal communications standard, such as SNA, DECNET, DCA, and ETHERNET. But for the user who has hardware from multiple vendors, or for different users who now want to communicate, the lack of basic communications standards creates serious problems. To complicate the situation further, there is also the issue of multinational networks. The OSI reference model is an attempt to provide a long-term solution to this problem. The reference model provides a common way of thinking about and organizing communications functions so that potential areas for standardization can be identified. Some of these areas were identified much earlier and already have standards, such as X.25 and X.21. Where this has happened, these existing standards will be integrated into the appropriate layer in the open system interconnection model. The OSI model is, however, much broader than any of these existing standards. Different communications systems will still implement functions differently; but with a common architecture and a well-defined set of standard interfaces, it will be much easier for these different systems to communicate with each other.

It is important that the reader who is interested in distributed database management systems be familiar with the basic concepts of the OSI model because they will affect the way communications systems are structured in many future distributed database management systems.

The OSI model uses the concept of layering. There are seven layers, which are discussed later on in more detail. The basic purpose of the layering is to provide a well-structured communications architecture. Each layer performs a set of closely related functions. The functions of one layer are invoked at the request of and to provide service to the layer above it. Two types of communications are involved in the model. The first type of communications, called an *interface*, is between two adjacent layers in the same processor. For example, there are interfaces between the application and presentation layers and between the transport and the network layers. *Protocols*, the second type of communications, exist between the same layer on different processors. For example, there are application-to-application protocols and session-to-session protocols. These protocols, which the ISO is trying to identify, define, and standardize, involve most of the communications across different types of systems. For performance reasons, some vendors may combine several layers into a single unit; but since they usually run within the same processor and are supplied by the same vendor, this should not create serious problems as long as they conform to the standard protocol for dealing with other systems.

The ISO had identified the following areas that must be addressed when different systems try to communicate with each other: interprocess communications, data representation, data storage, process management, resource management, integrity and security, and program support. To address these areas, the ISO has structured the communications system into seven layers: application, presentation, session, transport, network, data link, and physical. Each layer performs a certain specified set of functions. When necessary, a layer makes a request to the next lower layer for those services that it does not perform. The relationship of these layers and the two types of communications is shown in figure 3–2. Because in the past most of the work has been done at the lower layers, they are much better defined at this time. These lower layers represent the ''nuts and bolts'' of data communications, which any DDBMS takes for granted. The high layers, especially the application and presentation layers, are the ones that will have the most direct impact on DDBMS design and operation.

So far, the ISO has considered only those limited aspects of database management that directly and traditionally have affected the communications process. This is, in a sense, the reverse of the situation with the CODASYL Systems Committee, where most of the focus has been on the database management side, with much less concern for the data communications issues, although the committee did consider some of the basic communications requirements. In the future, the work of the two groups must be much more integrated.

The rest of this section briefly describes the functions of each of the seven layers. The top layer (layer 7)—the application layer—is the least well developed of the seven layers. It involves the basic application-to-application protocol. The application programs and some of the system software operate at this layer.

The next layer (layer 6) is the presentation layer. This layer performs three major functions to support the application layer: format management, transform management, and transformation performance. Format management determines which formats are involved, how to do the necessary transformations, and where they should be done. Until the data reach this level, the format is irrelevant to the OSI model. The lower levels are simply moving data, independent of their format. As a message is passed down through the various layers, each layer adds its own header information. To a lower layer, the headers of all the higher layers are simply part of the message that must be passed. Conversely, as a message is passed up through the layers, each layer strips off its own header information and passes the remaining message up to the next higher layer.

Transform management involves the format of the data while they are in the lower layers of the OSI model. It may be in some neutral OSI format. Data compression and encryption are two types of transformation the OSI may perform on the data independent of their format as defined by either of the two end systems.

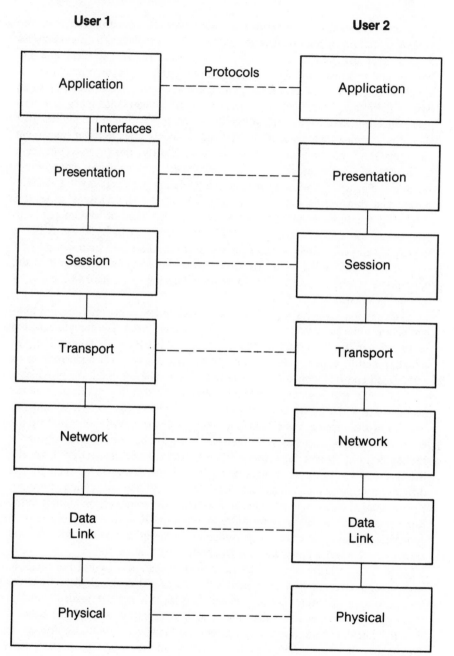

Figure 3–2. Open Systems Interconnection

Finally, transformation performance involves the synchronization of the various transform operations that are performed on the data. The main activity in this layer involves protocols for virtual terminals, virtual files, and job transfer and manipulation. The virtual terminal protocols involve mapping relatively small amounts of data between logical and physical terminals or between data in their stored form and the format required by particular types of terminals. Since this function is done at this level, the application at the higher layer should be terminal independent. Virtual file protocols involve the management and transfer of relatively large blocks of data. Clearly, this layer would seem to involve a significant set of data management and database management functions. Finally, the job transfer and manipulation protocols involve decomposing and transferring jobs among various systems. This is done at several levels. At the basic level, the user must know the type of system (and the appropriate job control language, or JCL) to and from which the job is being moved. At the two higher levels it is assumed that there will be a neutral OSI type of JCL that can be used. The software at this level should map it to the appropriate machine-specific JCL, thus providing improved hardware and system independence.

The session layer (layer 5) is the intermediate layer that provides the linkage between the presentation layer and the transport layer. The functions of the session layer are to establish the connections between an application/presentation entity, which represents an end user, and a physical node address as determined and maintained by the transport layer. The session layer provides a way to make this logical-to-physical mapping so that the application never needs to know the location of the process with which it is communicating. In fact, even the session layer is unconcerned with the physical location of the destination process. At any time there is a one-to-one relationship between a session connection and the corresponding transport layer connection. Over the life of a session, however, it may be connected and disconnected with several different transport connections; but there can be only one connection at a time. A presentation entity may be connected to many different session entities at the same time. Each of these connections is represented by one or more session connections. An application- or presentation-level entity also can have several simultaneous session connections with another application entity.

The session layer controls the flow of both data and control information. The session layer can function as a valve to accept or block data from the transport layer to ensure that the presentation layer is not overloaded. Finally, if the transport connection is lost, the session layer will reestablish the connection and carry out certain recovery procedures. However, it will also inform the presentation layer that the connection was lost and reestablished in case there are additional recovery procedures that must be done at the presentation or application layer.

The transport layer (layer 4) provides the data transfer service for the session layer. Each user/session entity has a unique identifier at the transport layer, but at this level it is a logical identifier rather than a physical address. Depending on their communications requirements, a specific user/session pair can have more than one actual path or connection. Furthermore, these different paths may be of different types.

The transport layer provides a connection, data transfer, and terminating phase. Examples of functions in the connection or establishment phase include selecting the most cost-effective type of network service and data-block size for the session, deciding whether or not to multiplex the transport-to-network connection, mapping the logical identifier at the transport layer into a physical address at the network layer, and setting up the necessary functions to be used during the subsequent data transfer phase. These transfer functions include blocking and segmenting of data, controlling the flow of both end-user data and control information, and detecting and recovering from errors. Finally, the termination phase involves breaking the connection in an orderly way so that no data are lost. In summary, most of the decisions concerning the cost and quality of the communications process are made at the transport layer based on the requirements specified by the higher layers.

The network layer (layer 3) provides the transport layer with point-to-point connections based on logical node identifiers. This allows the transport layer to remain independent of any routing or physical implementations issues in the communications system. If the message must be routed through several intermediate nodes, this is done automatically by the network layer. The transport layer can remain independent even if different parts of the path use very different technology such as fiber optics local loops, satellite links, or phone lines. The network layer moves network data units through the system and is unconcerned with the format of the data within these units. Network services are defined and implemented by a series of implementation-independent primitives. These primitives are then mapped into hardware-specific implementations at one of the two lower layers, the data link and the physical layers.

The purpose of the data link layer (layer 2) is to ensure the accurate transmission of data. It must check for any transmission errors or for lost data. To do this, the sending data link must break the message into manageable blocks or packets and assign indentifiers to them. The receiving data link module must check each packet for errors and reassemble the original message. At this time, it must also check to ensure that all of the parts of the message have been received. This error checking provides a certain minimal flow-control function. If it detects too many errors or determines that a communications path has failed, it can directly notify the next higher layer so that the path can be changed and the message rerouted.

There must be many different versions of the data-link-layer program modules because many of the functions at this layer are dependent on specific implementations of the communications systems. Examples of these dependencies include the communications-path type and bandwidth and the error detection and recovery procedures.

The physical layer (layer 1) is the most basic of the layers. It provides the basic mechanical and electrical connections between the terminal equipment and the communications circuit equipment. This layer is already well defined and has many widely accepted standards, such as EIA RS-232-C (for electrical), various pin connector standards (for mechanical), and X.21 (for precedural).

3–5. Summary

This chapter has provided a basic introduction to data communications. It began by discussing basic concepts, including bandwidth, mode, transfer rate, communications delay, and reliability. It discussed some of the communications technologies used for intracomputer communications, local networks, and conventional communications. It then reviewed the general communications architecture proposed by Anderson and Jensen. Finally, it described the open-system interconnection model being proposed by the International Standards Organization as the basis for future standards.

Notes

1. J. Martin, *Systems Analysis for Data Transmission* (Englewood Cliffs, N.J.: Prentice-Hall, 1972).

2. K.J. Thurber and H.A. Freeman, *Tutorial: Local Computer Network Architecture* (Long Beach, Calif.: IEEE Computer Society, 1980).

3. G.A. Anderson and E.D. Jensen, ''Computer Interconnection: Taxonomy, Characteristics, and Examples,'' *Computing Surveys* 7, no. 4 (December 1975).

4. International Organization for Standardization (ISO), *Open Systems Interconnection—Basic Reference Model,* ISO/TC 97/SC 16 (November 1980).

4 Distributed Processing

This chapter reviews the basic concepts of distributed processing and provides a bridge between the previous chapter on data communications and chapter 5 on distributed database management systems. Data communications are necessary for distributed processing. However, distributed processing encompasses far more than just data communications. Similarly, distributed database management systems are a very specific type of distributed processing. Therefore, in order to place distributed database management in the proper perspective, it is necessary to understand the broader concepts of distributed processing. That is the purpose of this chapter—to provide the broader perspective by reviewing the various concepts of distributed processing before narrowing the focus to a specific type of distributed processing: distributed database management.

This chapter consists of three sections. The first section discusses the objectives of distributed processing. The second identifies some underlying assumptions that determine the type of distributed system being considered. Knowing these assumptions is important because changing any one of them can drastically change the characteristics of the system. The third section describes a range of distributed system alternatives. In many cases these systems have evolved in a particular sequence because, as the technology developed, new distribution alternatives became feasible. The last and most complex of these alternatives is the generalized distributed database management system. This alternative leads directly into the next chapter, which provides a more detailed discussion of this alternative. Subsequent chapters then provide greater detail on specific aspects of distributed database management.

4–1. Distributed Processing Objectives

This section discusses the objectives of distributed processing. There are two basic types of objectives—organizational and technical. The most frequently discussed objectives are technical, but the organizational objectives may be even more important. The way to distinguish between organizational and technical objectives is to ask if the user at a terminal knows whether or not the system is distributed. If the user cannot tell, then the system was distributed for technical reasons, not organizational ones. If the user can tell the difference and must deal with the system differently depending on whether or not it is distributed, then the distribution decision was based on organizational factors.

49

The technical issues usually involve the distribution of hardware (processors and storage) and operations. This type of distribution should be completely transparent to the user. In this case distributed processing is simply the most effective way to meet the organization's objectives. For example, if a user needs a five-second response to a transaction, either a distributed or a centralized system could be used as long as the response time is met. On the other hand, organizational issues usually concern distributing other data processing functions, such as systems analysis, design, programming, maintenance, and management. For example, if a user wants direct control over the development activities and priorities, then the distribution of the analysis and programming staff may be required.

Organizational Objectives

The distribution of the hardware is only one of a series of distribution decisions that must be made. There are four distinct data processing functions that could be distributed: (1) systems analysis; (2) programming; (3) operations; and (4) planning, coordination, and management.

The first function is *systems analysis*. Is the analysis and design work done centrally, or is it distributed and located with the users in various remote sites? If the analysis is done by analysts who are located at the sites with the users, they may have a better understanding of the problem and develop better communications with the users. This closer contact can result in a better identification of the problems and more effective data processing solutions. This is especially true if the different sites have very different types of application. The disadvantage is that without clear and enforced design standards, the design methods and procedures at the various sites can diverge. This can create serious compatibility and maintenance problems later.

The second function that can be distributed is *programming*. Regardless of where the hardware is placed and where the systems analysis is done, there is still the question of where the programming is actually done. Given clear and complete design specifications, it makes little difference where the programming is done because the programmers should need very little direct interaction with the users. This, of course, does not apply when the analysis, design, and programming functions are combined in the same people. Currently there is some justification for centralizing the programming function because of economies of scale. A large central programming staff can include experts in many specific areas, such as operating systems, data communications, and database management. On the other hand, as ease of use becomes a more integral part of software systems design, the need for these specialists should decrease. This same ease of use trend will encourage more and more end users to become directly involved in the design and programming of their own applications. This trend is already apparent today in the use of end-user-oriented high-level query languages.

The third functional area is *operations*. The assumption is often made that distribution of the hardware requires distribution of the operations staff, but this is not necessarily the case. In many cases with remote turnkey systems the application can be down-loaded from the central site and any diagnostics can be dumped up line for maintenance and repair. In this case all the local personnel need to be able to do is turn the system on, replace the paper, and call the local maintenance personnel. In other words, some distributed hardware could be used just as typewriters and photocopies are used today in most offices.

In addition to the location of operations personnel in general, there is also a question of locating the data entry personnel. The guideline that the data should be captured as early as possible and as close to their origin as possible suggests that data entry should be done at the local site whenever possible. This approach also tends to improve the quality and timeliness of the data.

The fourth function is *planning and coordination*. Up to a point, this function must be centralized; otherwise, there would be little standardization or compatibility. This could lead to distributed systems in which the nodes could not communicate with each other and in which maintenance problems would be even worse than they are today. A compromise some organizations have made is to have a central data processing or planning and standards group select certain types of hardware and software that can be used in a distributed system. A technical decision can then be made on an application-by-application basis. If an application is distributed, it is composed of a standard set of building blocks. This minimizes the organization's later maintenance problems.

The most important organizational objective of distributed processing is to allow the user more direct control over what is being done. A manager is responsible for meeting certain objectives and should be given the necessary resources, including people, money, and information. In the past, managers have been given direct control of only the first two types of resources. Very rarely did they have direct control of the information resources and the equipment and personnel needed to provide that information. One of the benefits of distributed processing is to move these information resources out to the individual managers. This is usually the rationale for distributing the analysis, design, and programming functions. It is usually less important that the manager have a piece of hardware or direct control over the hardware. The driving force often comes from the lack of responsiveness of the current data processing department to the users' needs. If the data processing department is well organized and effectively meeting the requirements of the organization, then more direct control is probably not a major issue.

Technical Objectives

The main technical objectives of distributed processing are improved reliability, faster response time, lower costs, and increased performance. These objectives are only potential benefits of distributed processing. Depending on the nature of the application and the way the system is implemented, some of these potential benefits will be realized, whereas others will be sacrificed.

Improved reliability is one of the major objectives of distributed processing. System reliability is crucial if one of the applications (for example, airline reservations) is essential to the organization's continued operations. To some extent reliability can be provided by either a centralized or a distributed system. Multiprocessors and duplexed systems provide some improved reliability for the centralized approach. The emerging concern with disaster planning, however, makes any centralized system suspect. Even a duplexed system provides little reliability if a fire or other disaster destroys the data center.

Much greater reliability is provided by distributing the system to a number of different sites. Such a system has many nodes, with different users entering the system from different nodes. If one node fails, then only the users at that node are isolated and unable to use the system. The reliability and availability of the system is improved even more if users can enter the system from any node. Then the users who normally enter the system through the node that failed can be rerouted and enter through another node. If this rerouting is possible, then the failure of a node does not lock any user out of the system. All the users can still access the system and perform any function. The only result of a node failure in this case may be some performance degradation. Both these scenarios make an assumption about the design of the distributed system. They assume that any function or application can be performed at any of the nodes. A different design approach, however, could have each node dedicated to a specific set of functions. Requests for a function then would be sent to the appropriate node regardless of the node at which the user entered the system. In this case, when a node failed, unless its functions had been assigned to several nodes, they would not be available to any user anywhere in the system. This is the type of vulnerability exhibited by those distributed systems that rely on a major central node. This type of distributed processing does not necessarily improve the reliability of the system. If, on the other hand, any node can perform any function, then as long as one node remains available, the system can continue to do any function. The distributed system with the greatest reliability is the one that allows users to enter at any node and in which any node can perform any function. In this case, the failure of a node simply reduces the capacity of the system but does not reduce the system's functionality or lock out any user.

The last reliability issue involves data availability. If the only copy of the data a user needs is stored at the failed node, then the improved reliability is an illusion. An integral part of improved reliability must be data redundancy. Therefore, if a distributed system is to have high reliability, its design must ensure that the failure of a node or a communications path does not isolate either a user or the only copy of any of the data and that no single failure prevents any function from being performed.

The next two objectives, faster response time and lower costs, are related because both are affected by how much the communications system is used. If there is high locality of reference—that is, certain parts of the data are used primarily by one node—then the data can be stored at the node at which they are most often used. In this case, the data usually will be processed locally. This leads to improvements in both response time and costs because the use of the communications system is minimized. (This assumes, of course, that the communications system is slow and expensive, which is usually the case today.) If there is not high locality of reference, then these response time and cost improvements are unlikely. If most of the requests involve retrievals, however, some benefits are still possible even without locality of reference. Replicating the data at each node would still allow retrievals to be done locally. Although this redundancy would increase the storage costs, it would provide faster response time and lower costs because at least the retrievals could still be done locally. The problem would be with the update synchronization that would be required to keep the copies of the data consistent. If there were many updates, this synchronization overhead would more than eliminate any benefits that would be obtained by being able to do the retrievals locally. (Chapter 8 discusses this synchronization problem in more detail.)

The last technical objective of distributed processing involves the long-term growth of the system. Distributed processing provides a way—in some cases the only way—to increase the performance of an organization's data processing system. Because an organization's data processing requirements increase, the power of its current system eventually must also be increased. The usual approach is to upgrade to a larger computer within the same family. This minimizes the conversion problems. With the centralized system, however, these upgrades may still be a traumatic experience, especially if they involve any hardware incompatibilities or require major changes in the system software. Thus upgrading a large centralized system can still occasionally create problems. On the other hand, in a well-designed distributed system incremental growth is relatively easy because any number of additional nodes can be added to increase the overall system capacity to almost any level. In some cases this is an easier growth path than is upgrading a large central system. However, the initial step from a central system to a distributed one can be very difficult.

The foregoing discussion assumes that modular growth through a family of computers is at least a possibility. This is not the case, however, if the organization is already using the largest system in the family. In this situation the organization has two choices. The first is to convert to a different, more powerful family (assuming one exists). Unfortunately, this alternative usually results in major conversion problems. The second alternative is to add another computer—that is, increase the overall power of the system by adding computers rather than by upgrading. Once an organization has more than one computer, the next logical step is to connect them into a distributed system.

The only way this can be avoided is if the applications can be partitioned into two completely independent sets with no data overlap. Any data overlap forces the systems to be integrated into a distributed system. In summary, distributed processing is the only way in which system performance can always be increased. In some cases, upgrading provides an alternate growth path, but distributed processing is the only way to increase performance above a certain maximum.

In summary, there are many objectives for distributed processing, only some of which may be realized in any specific system. In most cases in the past, the technical, cost-effectiveness objectives have been the driving force. These objectives include improved reliability and response time, lower costs, and increased performance or system growth. In some cases, however, organizational rather than technical factors have been the driving force. The main organizational objective is improved management control. In the future this organizational objective probably will be the key factor in many distribution decisions. In fact, in some cases an organization may select a distributed system for the improved management control, even though it is more expensive than the equivalent centralized system. The improved control may be more important than the added costs. When the organizational factors are forcing a distribution decision, various data processing functions such as analysis and programming may be distributed in addition to—or even instead of—the hardware.

4–2. Distributed System Architectural Assumptions

There are many approaches to distributed processing. Discussing the "best" type of distributed system is like determining the "best" programming language: any such evaluation depends on many factors. This is one reason there are so many different approaches to distributed processing. Underlying each approach is a set of critical assumptions about the characteristics of the problem to be solved and the system necessary to solve it. In many descriptions of specific distributed systems these assumptions and their effects are implicit. For clarity, they should be stated explicitly along with a systematic discussion of how varying them affects the design and performance of the distributed system. It is important to understand the types of assumptions that must be made and to be able to make the necessary trade-offs.

Changing the assumptions or characteristics of a distributed system can have two types of effects. In the first, simpler case, the change affects the value of one or more parameters in the model of the distributed system. Although modification of the parameter may drastically change a preferred design alternative, these variations are relatively easy to include in an analysis. The second, more complex case occurs when the change modifies or invalidates a basic premise of a design algorithm and forces the entire model to be restructured. For example, relaxing the constraint that data cannot be replicated, to allow arbitrary replication, completely changes the way updates must be handled. Algorithms that were correct in the former case are incorrect and produce invalid results when the constraint is relaxed. There are various assumptions or constraints concerning data distribution, communications, the data model and language, and the characteristics of the application for which the system was designed. Collectively these factors determine the type of distributed system architecture that is possible and the range of viable solutions to the specific problem.

Data Distribution

The first constraint concerns the type of data distribution the system supports. When data are stored at many nodes, replication becomes an issue. If there is no overlap in the data, the distributed system is much simpler because without replication there are no multiple copies to synchronize. Other requirements, such as reliability, could force the data to be fully replicated—that is, a complete copy of all of the data at every node. A more flexible approach would allow the data to be replicated arbitrarily with any amount of overlap. Each of these data distribution alternatives requires a different type of distributed system and a different set of update algorithms. In other words, when a specific distributed system is described, built into its design is an implicit decision about the type of data distribution that is allowed. Various types of data distribution assumptions are discussed in more detail in chapter 6 ("Data Distribution") and 8 ("Update Synchronization").

Communications

In designing a distributed system, many trade-offs must be made between communications and local processing and storage. The way in which these trade-offs should be made is based on the relative characteristics of the communications and the processing subsystems. Most distributed processing work today makes a common assumption about the communications system that links the nodes. This assumption is that there is a low- to moderate-bandwidth communications system that links the nodes. This communications system has a long time delay, at least in relation to processor speeds. In this case the trade-off between communications costs and delays, on the one hand, and processing costs, on the other, is clear. Whenever possible, cheap, fast, local processing and storage should be used to minimize the costs and delays incurred by the communications system—that is, to minimize the amount of communications. These trade-offs become even more important if the communications system involves very low bandwidth, long-delay dial-up lines. At the other extreme, if the communications is through shared memory or very high bandwidth fiber optics (as in a local network), then the trade-offs could be very different. In these cases communications could be cheaper and faster than local processing and storage. Much of the work with local computer networks is moving toward these very high speed communications subsystems. In fact, one can imagine breakthroughs in communications technology that would reverse the trend that now favors distributed processing. After all, it was not long ago that processor costs made distributed processing too expensive to be feasible.

Data Models and Languages Supported

A third factor in distributed systems design is the data model and the data manipulation language supported by the system. The capability to transfer a file between nodes is a first step in the distributed direction. In a sense, a file transfer request is a high-level query because it does specify all the data that are needed, so that the system can optimize how to perform the operation. Unfortunately, such a simple request usually results in transferring far more data than are really needed. Considering the usual characteristics of the communications system, this can seriously degrade the system's performance. This type of distributed file system is much simpler than a distributed database management system but not nearly as flexible. With distributed database management systems, the data model and the data manipulation language can drastically affect system complexity, flexibility, and performance. With a high-level, nonprocedural query language, the distributed database management system knows much more about the nature of the request and can do more optimization. Depending on the purpose of the system, an algorithm can be selected to optimize any one of several performance factors, such as response time, throughput, total processing time, or total cost to process the query. On the other hand, with low-level, record-at-a-time data manipulation languages, which force the user to do his or her own navigation through the data structure, the system can do little optimizing. In this case the communications load on the system can become intolerable. The language level does not really change the type of question the user can ask. Any high-level query can always be decomposed into an equivalent series of low-level queries. In terms of performance, this means that it may not be possible to distribute a CODASYL-based database management system effectively unless it includes a high-level, nonprocedural data manipulation language. This is not a serious problem, however, because most such system already include a high-level query capability.

Type of Application

Most distributed systems, especially distributed database management systems so far, have been developed for a specific type of application. Implicit in their design, therefore, is an assumption about the characteristics of the applications they can process. Major application characteristics include database size, transaction volume, volume of data each transaction requires from the database, relative frequency of retrievals as opposed to updates, complexity of the transactions, and locality of reference.

The key point is that different types of distributed systems are needed for different types of problems. Depending on the type of problem, there are different sets of requirements and constraints. There is simply no "best" distributed system design that can be used for all types of problems.

Some type of model or analysis method is necessary to allow the system designer to study the trade-offs among the various alternatives. Today there are many different models. However, each one examines only a small part of the complete systems design problem. There is a set of models to analyze the data placement. There is another set of models to analyze the performance of various update synchronization algorithms. There is a third set to study query decomposition. Subsequent chapters on each of these areas discuss the characteristics of the models for each area. Unfortunately, the linkages are missing. Models are developed to analyze the trade-offs in a specific area, but rarely are the models linked to study the trade-off among different areas. A data placement decision affects the performance of the update synchronization algorithms, which in turn affect how a particular query should be decomposed and processed. Such an integrating model does not exist today.

4–3. Distributed Processing Alternatives

Before concentrating on distributed database management systems, consider the range of distributed processing alternatives that exists today. An organization can select any one of many distributed processing alternatives. At one extreme there is the centralized approach, in which both the processing power and the data storage are centralized. At one time this was the only option available, and in certain cases it is still the most cost effective approach. Now, however, there is a broad range of hardware distribution alternatives. The distribution of I/O devices allows either remote job entry (RJE) or transaction processing, depending on the type of I/O device. In either case the processing is still done by the central site. The use of intelligent terminals, microcomputers, minicomputers, or even additional mainframes permits the distribution of processing power. Finally, nodes may include secondary storage devices either for temporary storage, as with data entry, or for permanent storage for local copies or partitions of a database. Each of these alternatives is considered in more detail later.

An important point must be made about all these alternatives. A distribution option relates to a specific application. A large organization has many applications, such as order entry, inventory control, billing, and payroll. Different applications could be implemented using different distribution alternatives. For example, payroll may only use transaction processing with very minimal local editing, whereas order entry may use distributed data entry with extensive local editing, and inventory control may be implemented to allow the local sites to communicate with each other. As more sophisticated alternatives are used, the system software must provide more support functions. Once the support for a given level of distribution is provided, that level or any lower level can be implemented. The lower levels simply would not use all the support facilities provided in the system software. Usually, once a system is enhanced, most of the new applications would make use of the new features it provides. Applications developed before the enhancements, however, would not use them. Therefore, at any time an organization could have various applications using different levels of distribution. The most complex approach, which subsumes all the previous alternatives, involves distributed database management systems.

Centralized Processing and Storage with Remote Job Entry

When computers were first introduced, all the processing, storage, and I/O had to be done at the central site. The first type of hardware that was distributed was the I/O device. Initially, only the card readers and printers were distributed, with a minimal amount of local processing. This permitted RJE. No longer was it necessary to hand deliver card decks and printouts to and from the central site. Now, programs and data submitted at various local sites would be read and transmitted to the central site for processing. Then the output would be transmitted back to the local site. This improved the turnaround time for the jobs, which were all still submitted and done on a batch basis.

    The next step in the evolution of distributed processing occurred when a different type of I/O device was introduced. This was the terminal, which could be used for on-line and transaction processing.

Centralized Processing and Storage with On-Line Terminals
for Transaction Processing

With this approach, all the processing and storage resources are still centralized. Each user location has one or more terminals connected to the central site. The number of terminals at each location depends on the amount of activity. In principle, a user at any location can invoke any of the functions at the central site. If there is very little activity at a particular location, its requests may be forwarded to the central site in a noncomputer form—for example, a telephone call or a letter. The operations staff at the central site could then invoke the function and send the results back. This would be the case if the amount of activity did not justify a terminal and the communications lines. Because of declining hardware costs and increasing user expectations, this situation is less common today than it was in the past. It now takes relatively little activity to justify a local terminal. As the activity at the node increases, additional terminals and communications lines can be added. Increases in the workload at a node or the addition of new nodes to the network do not change the basic architecture for this distributed approach. The communications costs for this approach, however, are relatively high because all the requests and data have to be transmitted to and from the central site for each transaction. To minimize this communications cost, some functions, such as data entry, can be shifted from the central site to the local sites.

*Centralized Processing and Storage with Distributed Data
Entry*

The previous approach used very simple terminals with little or no intelligence. This approach adds a minimal amount of processing and storage capacity (such as an intelligent terminal or a local microprocessor) at some nodes to permit local data entry and editing. Most of the data entry and editing is then done locally by local personnel. This activity requires no data communications until the editing is completed. Once the data have been edited and are ready to be entered and processed, they are transmitted to the central site and the permanent files or database is updated.

In some systems the transactions are transmitted to the central site individually as soon as they have been edited, but in other cases the transactions are temporarily stored at the local site and transmitted as a batch. The latter approach requires additional local storage. When a transaction or a batch of transactions is received at the central site, it may be processed immediately or the processing may be delayed, either until a larger batch of transactions has been accumulated or until a scheduled processing time.

Some of the processing at the central site may involve further editing, at one of four levels. First, there is *item* or *field-level editing*. This verifies that the value for each field in the transaction is acceptable—for example, that salary is numeric or that the specified credit code is one of a set of predefined codes. Second, there is the *transaction* or *interfield-level edit*. This checks the values in several fields for consistency—for example, if a sale is to be charged, the account number must be specified. The third level is the *batch level,* which involves various control information that is attached to the batch as it moves through the system. These first three levels can be checked locally. The fourth level is the *database level*. These edits require access to the database. They determine whether the transaction is consistent with data already in the data-base—for example, ensuring the uniqueness of a new customer number.

Distributed Data Entry and Editing with a Local Partition of the Central Database

This approach is a relatively simple extension of the previous one. It provides additional local storage at the node. Part of the database is temporarily stored at the node for more complete editing. In this case all the editing, including the fourth level, can be done entirely at the local site. This delays the point at which the node must communicate with the central site. Only when the node is completely satisfied with the data is it sent to the central site. With this and the foregoing alternatives, all the processing, except for data entry and editing, is done at the central site. This approach minimizes the amount of processing needed at each of the local nodes, but it also reduces the amount of communications that is needed.

An important point with this approach is that part of the database is stored locally only for editing purposes. All the actual processing and updating is still done at the central site. The local copy is only a snapshot of part of the database at a particular point in time. It is not updated when the central database is modified. Therefore, this approach is appropriate only in certain specialized editing situations.

There are two obvious ways this approach can be enhanced. First, any node that has enough processing power and storage for this alternative can also be used for transactions processing. Also, any local editing that is being done for input, can also be done for output. Only a software constraint would prevent this level of distribution from being used for either editing or transaction processing. In fact, given this distribution of hardware with the appropriate software, some functions (such as inventory control, billing, and order entry) could be done centrally, using only transaction processing, whereas other functions could be using the local data entry and editing capability.

The second type of enhancement would involve allowing the local node actually to process its local copy of the database. The complex update synchronization problem is avoided if the local copy is treated as a snapshot at a certain point in time. For certain applications up-to-the-second synchronization of copies is not essential. This enhancement, however, leads to the next alternative, wherein part of the database is permanently stored locally.

Distributed Processing and Storage with the Local Sites Linked to the Central Site

In this case the node has local processing power but may also have a significant amount of secondary storage so that data and programs can be permanently stored locally. This approach is most appropriate when each local site needs to perform certain functions on its own data. An example is an inventory system in which each warehouse stores and maintains its own inventory data. In this case all the nodes are doing the same operations on the same type of data, but the approach would be the same if some of the nodes in the system were sales offices processing their own customer or order data. Periodically, the updates would be sent to the central site to update the corporate records, but most of the activity is done locally. Note that the key point is not the function that is being done but rather the location at which it is performed. These same functions could have been done centrally using transaction processing.

This approach involves relatively little communications between a local site and the central site. However, this statement only applies to the function for which this alternative is being used. If there is another function at the local site that has been implemented using transaction processing, then for that function there would be extensive communications. There is also little or no communications among the local sites. Any communication is between a local site and the central system, not between various local sites. The next alternative removes this restriction.

Distributed Processing and Storage with Local Sites
Interconnected

A logical extension of the foregoing case is to allow the various local sites to communicate with each other. For example, if a warehouse has an order to ship 100 widgets but has only 50 in stock, it may request that another warehouse ship the remaining 50. This could be done in the previously described system by sending the request back to the central site, which would then issue the request to the second warehouse. There are some benefits, including reduced communications, in allowing the local sites to communicate with each other. The trade-off is that this may add some complexity to the system design. In most cases, with this type of system, the user has to know where the data are and how to access them. Systems at this stage of development do not have the sophisticated support software to determine where the data are located and to access them automatically. Adding this layer of complexity is part of what moves the system into the last category, the distributed database management system. The difference in these two approaches can be shown using the foregoing example. The distributed database management system approach would allow the user to ask for a warehouse with at least 100 widgets in stock. The system would then query many local sites to find one that had enough widgets and could then request that warehouse to make the entire shipment. The system has done a significant amount of work, but the user may have issued only one request to ship 100 widgets. Without the capability of a distributed database management system, the user would have had to ask each of the warehouses specifically, one at a time, whether it had enough widgets. When he found one that did, he could request that warehouse to fill the order. Obviously, in both cases the result is the same—100 widgets are shipped—but in one case the system did most of the work for the user, whereas in the other case the user had to do most of the work himself.

Distributed Database Management System

This approach involves the greatest level of software support. The user should be able to access data anywhere within the system without being forced to specify its location. For performance reasons, most of the transactions in this type of system should use high-level, nonprocedural query languages so that the system can optimize the necessary processing and communications. Even with this approach, there are many different levels at which the system could support the user. A particular distributed database design may or may not allow replicated data. The most general case, however, would allow an arbitrary degree of data replication, which would require precedures to maintain the consistency among the various copies of the data.

The next chapter introduces the new concepts required for database management in a distributed environment. The components of a distributed database management system (DDBMS) are described. There is also a discussion of the functions a DDBMS must perform and how these functions can be distributed through the system. Subsequent chapters focus on specific technical aspects of distributed database management, such as data placement, function placement, update synchronization, and query decomposition. Finally, the concluding chapter makes some projections about the future of distributed database technology.

5

Distributed Database Management Concepts

This chapter introduces and explains the new concepts required to move database management into a distributed environment. The first section describes the basic operation of a database in a distributed environment and identifies and explains the components of a distributed database management system. The CODASYL distributed database report identified three types of components— user related, data related, and network related. These components may be either data or procedures that use the data. The user-related and data-related components in a distributed database management system (DDBMS) are the same as those in a centralized DBMS. The user-related components are the user, the user process, and the subschema. The data-related components include the database, the schema, and the DBMS procedures. The network-related components are the new ones that must be added because of the distributed environment. Therefore, most of the chapter focuses on these network-related components. The second section of the chapter discusses four types of distribution: centralized, replicated, partitioned, and hybrid. Any of the components, either data or procedures, can be distributed using any of the four approaches. This section discusses the distribution alternatives in general because chapters 6 and 7 deal with these distribution alternatives in more detail, specifically for data and function distribution. The third section describes the distribution of the various DDBMS components.

5–1. DDBMS Operations and Components

This section describes and explains the various distributed database management system components, with most of the emphasis on the new network-related components. It begins by briefly describing how a DDBMS operates and how the components fit together, but without considering how they might be distributed. Later sections of this chapter and the following chapters indicate many possible distribution alternatives. Therefore, an actual system would be much more complex.

For this discussion, consider the system shown in figure 5–1. Each node, such as a warehouse, has all the components of a DDBMS, but the local database is different at each node—that is, the database has been partitioned so that each node or warehouse has its own local inventory data. To determine how many widgets the company has in its entire inventory, the user issues a

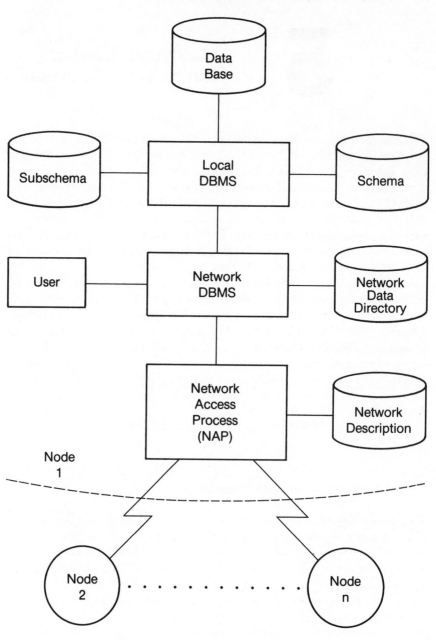

Figure 5–1. Components of a DDBMS

high-level request that is accepted and initially processed by the network database management system (NDBMS). The NDBMS uses the network data directory to determine where the inventory data for widgets are stored. There are three possible results, each of which involves a different type of processing.

The first alternative is that all the widgets are stored in the local warehouse. This means that the inventory data are all at the local node. Therefore, all the NDBMS has to do is pass the request to the local DBMS, which uses its schema to locate and retrieve the data. It then uses the subschema to map the data into the form expected by the user. This response is then passed back to the NDBMS, which in turn passes it to the user.

The second alternative is that all the widgets and their inventory data are stored at one of the other nodes. The request is still initially processed by the NDBMS, but it must use the network data directory to determine where the requested data are stored and to determine the appropriate logical node identifier. The NDBMS then passes the request and the logical node identifier to the network access process (NAP). The NAP—that is, the communications software—uses the network description to convert the logical identifier into a physical node address and to route the request. At the destination node the NAP accepts the request and passes it on to the NDBMS, which in turn passes it on to the local DBMS. The local DBMS then uses its schema to locate and retrieve the data. The data must then be converted into the form the user expects. This may be done using the local subschema. However, this conversion could be deferred and done later when the data are returned to the user's node. In either case the local DBMS passes the response back through the NDBMS to the NAP, which transmits it back to the user's node. To return the data requested, the NDBMS specifies the logical node identifier to which the response should be sent. The NDBMS can do this simply by remembering the node from which the request came. It does not need to use the network data directory. The NAP maps the logical node identifier into a physical node address and routes the message back to the user's node. At the user's node the message is received by the NAP and passed on to the NDBMS. If the request has already been converted into the form expected by the user, then the NDBMS would simply pass the response back to the user. If the user's subschema is stored locally and the conversion is done at this point, then the NDBMS passes the response data back to the local DBMS for the necessary conversion. The local DBMS does the conversion and passes the converted data back to the NDBMS, which finally returns the response to the user.

The third alternative is that widgets are in the inventory of several of the warehouses. However, the request is for the total number of widgets in the company's inventory, not simply the number of widgets in any specific warehouse. In this case, when the NDBMS begins to process the request, it discovers that the request must be sent to several destination nodes. The process for each destination node is the same as was just described. The difference occurs when the responses are returned to the NDBMS at the user's node. The NDBMS knows that it is going to get responses from several nodes, including a possible response from the local DBMS, which is treated exactly like any other node. All these responses are then consolidated into the single response that the user expects, in this case the sum of the number of widgets in the inventory of all the warehouses.

The complexity of the requests that the DDBMS will accept determines the sophistication required by the NDBMS in evaluating and selecting network-wide processing strategies and in consolidating the responses. The foregoing example involved a relatively simple request and range of data distribution alternatives. However, it does provide an illustration of how the various parts of the DDBMS are related. With this overview as a background, the rest of this section describes the various components of the DDBMS in more detail. Descriptions of still more complex alternatives are provided in later chapters.

The CODASYL report identifies four new network-related components in a distributed environment. Two of these components are data, and two are sets of procedures that use these new data components. These four components are the network description, the network access process, the network data directory, and the network database management system. These components are described here, beginning with the low-level communications-related components.

First, there is the network access process (NAP). The NAP is the communications software linking the node to the rest of the distributed system. It performs most of the basic communications functions. These are the functions performed by the lower four or five layers in the open system interconnection architecture—that is, the physical, data link, network, transport, and session layers. Although these procedures are new in the database area, all communications systems are already performing most of these functions. One of the significant tasks remaining in the distributed database area is to determine how to relate and interface the various database management and data-communications functions effectively.

The second network component is the network description. This component defines the network—which nodes exist and how they are connected. The network description provides a detailed definition of each node and the paths linking them. The node definition may include the node type, its processing power, its memory size, its secondary storage capacity, and the functions and procedures that can be executed on the node. Similarly, the path definition identifies the nodes that are connected to each other and defines the type of link, its bandwidth, and the required protocols. At a minimum the network description must include enough information for the NAP to determine how to route messages among the various nodes. The network description identifies the physical nodes and the various paths that link them. The mapping between logical node identifiers and the physical node addresses, which are used by the lower layers of the communications software for routing, must be done at a higher level.

The network data directory (NDD), the third network-related component, provides the data necessary to determine the logical node identifier. From the data specified in the request, the NDBMS must determine the logical node identifiers to which various parts of a request can be sent. The network data directory can be relatively simple or very complex, depending on how the database has been distributed. For example, the database may be distributed using data-item partitioning. This means that by knowing the data item that is needed, the NDBMS can determine where to send the request. All data items of a particular type are stored at a specific node. In other words, all the employee data are at one node, whereas all inventory data are at another and all customer data at still another node. In this case, the network data directory needs only schema-level information. Alternatively, the data could be partitioned by data value. An example of this approach is found where each warehouse has its own inventory data. In this case, schema-level information does not uniquely determine where the data is stored. The network data directory must include both schema and data-value information. Still another complication arises when the data are replicated. Now there must be a network data-directory entry for each copy of the data. In many cases the various copies are indistinguishable; however, in some cases, as with dominant-copy synchronization, the various copies may have different characteristics that the network data directory must also record.

The final network-related component is the network database management system (NDBMS). The NDBMS performs five functions, some of which are required because of the distributed environment, others of which existed even in a centralized environment, although they were done differently. These five functions are described here.

First, the NDBMS provides the interface between the user and the rest of the system. Since the user may request data stored at another node, the NDBMS rather than the local DBMS must be the first component to process the request. The local DBMS in a distributed system is the equivalent of the DBMS in a centralized system. However, the local DBMS does not know data exist at other nodes because it knows nothing about the rest of the network. Therefore, the NDBMS must initially accept the request from the user and analyze it to determine where the data are stored.

This is the second NDBMS function—to locate the data. It uses the network data directory to determine the logical identifier of the node at which the data are stored. If the request is for data that are stored locally, then the NDBMS simply passes it to the local DBMS, which can process it. If the request cannot be satisfied locally, then the NDBMS must do further analysis to identify and select a network-wide strategy for processing the request.

This selection of a network-wide strategy is the third function of the NDBMS. The types of requests the DDBMS allows determines the complexity of the strategy-selection function. There are two basic types of requests that cannot be satisfied locally. One type is the *remote request,* which must be sent to another node for processing. Once there, however, the request can be processed completely at that single node. In this case, determining the request strategy is very simple. The NDBMS only needs to determine the node to which to send the request. The other type of request is the *compound request,* with which the strategy selection becomes more complex because no single node can process the request completely. In this case the strategy selection involves decomposing the request into a set of local and remote requests that can be used to process the original request. There are many types of compound requests. One measure of the sophistication of a DDBMS is the range of compound requests it can process. The type of compound request determines both how the request can be decomposed (see chapter 9) and which update synchronization protocols can be used (see chapter 8).

The fourth function of the NDBMS is to provide network-wide backup procedures and, when necessary, to initiate and control network-wide recovery. Improved reliability is one of the major reasons for selecting a distributed system. Therefore, adequate backup and recovery procedures are essential. Given the necessary set of commands, the local DBMS can do the recovery of the local part of the database. The NDBMS, however, must decide which commands are necessary and then issue them to one or more of the local DBMSs. For example, if the local copy of the database is damaged and must be recovered, the local DBMS can do the recovery. While it is doing this, many other updates will probably be processed by other nodes in the network. Therefore, even after the local DBMS has completed its recovery, the local copy of the database may be out of date. The NDBMS must provide the local DBMS with the transactions that have been processed while the recovery was in progress. These transactions are necessary to bring the local database back up to date. Only after the database has been brought back up to date has it been fully recovered. Since the local DBMS is not aware that the network exists, it cannot control this part of the recovery. There are many ways in which a DDBMS can fail. All these cases must be considered, and the necessary actions must be assigned to either the NDBMS or the local DBMS. Chapter 8, which discusses update synchronization, has an extensive discussion of backup and recovery procedures for each of the synchronization procedures.

The final function of the NDBMS, the translation function, is required only in a heterogeneous system. Different nodes may have different hardware, different software (local DBMSs), or both. Just as data placement should be transparent to the user, so this heterogeneity should also be transparent. If this transparency is provided, it is the NDBMS that must do the necessary translation. Obviously, a homogeneous system with the same hardware and software at all the nodes is the simplest situation. Different hardware, but all of it using the same software, is the next simplest situation. Ideally, in this case the translation is primarily limited to word lengths and character codes. There may be some additional translation problems, however, because the same DBMS may be implemented slightly differently on different hardware. Either of these two translation problems is manageable with today's data-translation technology. The translation problem becomes much more difficult when the DBMSs are significantly different, in which case three types of translation are required. First, the request in one query language must be translated into the corresponding request (or the equivalent set of requests) in the other query language. This problem can be minimized by using a generic or neutral data manipulation language that can easily be translated into a query language for any of several different data models. Ideally, this approach involves a high-level query language. The second type of translation involves mapping from the data model and data structure of one DBMS to the corresponding structure and model of the other DBMS. Again, using a common or neutral data model, this can also be done. The third type of translation that may be necessary is the relatively simple translation from one set of hardware to another. Theoretically, these types of translation between heterogeneous DBMSs can be done. However, considering the various ways in which specific DBMSs are implemented, it is very difficult to develop any general purpose translator. Therefore, when it is done at all, this type of translation between DBMSs is usually done on an ad hoc basis.

5–2. Distribution Alternatives

This section discusses the basic distribution alternatives, which can be applied to either data or functions. The data in a DDBMS include not only the database but also the schema, the subschemas, the network data directory, and the network description. All these components can be distributed using any of the alternatives described in this section. Everyone recognizes that data can be distributed, but there has been much less consideration of how to distribute functions. Although there has been some discussion of how to distribute applications software and its data, there has been less discussion about distributing various parts of the system software and its supporting data. The next two chapters discuss data and function distribution in more detail. The purpose of this section is to provide an introduction and background for those two chapters. All four of the alternatives discussed here—centralized, replicated, partitioned, and hybrid—can be applied to either data or functions. The next section discusses these distribution alternatives in terms of the various DDBMS components.

The first placement alternative is to centralize a component. Most of the DDBMS components described here could be centralized. This could include, for example, the database and the DBMS that manages it. Until recently this was the only alternative that existed—the database and the DBMS were centralized, and only the users were distributed. This created several problems, however. Because of the extensive use of communications, both the costs and the response times of the system were increased. In many cases, however, the reliability and availability of the database was an even more crucial factor. Any component of the system that is centralized creates serious reliability problems. To avoid these problems, several distribution alternatives are possible.

Replication is the most obvious alternative. A complete copy of a component, such as the database or the DBMS, is placed at every node. This can result in major improvements in the reliability of the system. For retrievals, replication of the database also lowers the communications costs and reduces the response time. For updates, however, it creates serious complications because all the copies of the data must be synchronized. An important design factor in deciding whether or not to replicate data is the relative frequency of updates to retrievals. As a general rule, high percentages of updates suggest that there should be few copies of the data, because reducing the number of copies reduces the amount of synchronization overhead. This overhead is more serious when data are replicated than when various DDBMS processes or software are replicated. This is because of the relative frequency with which changes are made to the various DDBMS components. For example, if the network data directory is replicated, the copies must still be kept synchronized, but this creates less of a problem than replicating the database. Because the network data directory is rarely changed, the synchronization overhead is less of a performance problem. If software (such as the NAP or the NDBMS) is replicated, the synchronization problem is even smaller. The problem still exists because the software is occasionally changed, but this occurs only when one or more of the nodes convert to a new version of the software. This is a special situation and does not affect the normal operation of the system. Therefore, the synchronization problem can be ignored for the software. This is probably the reason most of the discussions about distribution—and particularly replication—focus on the data. The reason that system software, such as the NDBMS and the local DBMS, is usually replicated is that it is often used by all the nodes but is rarely modified. This means a very high retrieval-to-update ratio, so synchronization overhead is not a serious problem.

The third distribution alternative, partitioning, minimizes the synchronization problem, even for data that are frequently updated. With partitioning, a single copy of the data—whether it is the database or the network data directory or the network description—is divided into disjoint sets with each part of it being placed at different nodes. Since there is no overlap, there is only one copy of the data. This means that there is no consistency problem. Synchronization only becomes a problem with some compound requests that require data from several nodes. If the data are partitioned properly and certain types of requests are not allowed, the synchronization problem can be completely avoided. Partitioning is practical only if the data exhibit a high locality of reference. *Locality of reference* means that most of the requests for a particular part of the data come from a single node at which the data can be stored. Requests for that part of the data from other nodes are much less frequent. If all the nodes are equally likely to use the data, then partitioning would simply increase the amount of communications as all the nodes without a copy of the data tried to access them. The same point applies to partitioning the software. In most cases system software should not be partitioned. For example, all the nodes need access to the NAP, which, therefore, should be replicated rather than partitioned. Only in those cases in which different system functions are centralized at different nodes is their partitioning a viable option. Some application programs, however, may be used only at a specific node. In this case the application software may be partitioned, with different parts being stored at the nodes at which they are primarily used.

The final distribution alternative is a hybrid approach wherein different components or different parts of a component are placed using different distribution alternatives. For example, some of the database may be replicated if it is frequently used by all the nodes. Other parts of the data that are used primarily by only one node are placed at that node—that is, partitioned. Still other data that are frequently updated may be centralized to minimize the update synchronization overhead. Similarly, various software components can be placed using different alternatives. Not only applications software, but also some of the DDBMS system software, may also be distributed in different ways. Many of the larger nodes may have a complete set of the NDBMS and DBMS software, but some of the smaller nodes may have only parts of this support software. For example, a node may have a small part of the database and only retrieval routines so that it can be used for local queries but not for updating. Various alternatives for distributing the software are considered in more detail in chapter 7.

5–3. Distribution of the DDBMS Components

This section discusses the distribution of the specific DDBMS components. The components that are considered include the database, the database definition, the network data directory, the NDBMS, and the DBMS. The first three components are all data. The only differences among them are in how they are used and who has access to them. The last two components are processes or sets of functions. Data and function distribution are discussed in more detail in chapters 6 and 7, but this section describes some of the basic points.

The database is the first thing most people think of distributing when they consider a distributed database management system. Database distribution involves two levels of decisions. First, the distribution alternative must be selected. If the centralized or replicated alternative is selected, then the decision process is complete. If, however, the partitioned or hybrid approach is selected, then a second set of decisions must be made. More detailed design decisions are then required to decide which parts of the database to place where. Some of these design algorithms are described in the next chapter.

The decision about how to place the database cannot be made independently. It affects and is affected by the placement decisions for other components. If part of the database is placed at a node, then part of the database definition also must be placed there. This includes at a minimum the physical definition and the information necessary to retrieve the data. Similarly, enough of the DBMS functions must also be placed there to retrieve and process the database and its definition. The network data directory can be placed independently of the database and its definition. Its placement, however, is closely related to the placement of the various NDBMS functions that must use it. Therefore, although in principle placement decisions for the various components can be made independently, in practice many of these decisions must be made jointly.

The distribution decision for one component may seriously complicate another component. For example, if the database is to be partitioned, it can be divided by data item or by data value. The way in which the partitioning is done affects the complexity of the network data directory and that part of the NDBMS that uses it. With data-item partitioning different items are placed at different nodes; therefore, the network data directory needs only schema level data—that is, data-item names. If the partitioning is done by data value, then the network data directory must consider both data-item name and value. This will result in a much larger and more complicated network data directory, and this added complexity will be reflected in some of the NDBMS functions. Furthermore, if the hybrid approach is used, there will be multiple network data directory entries for some parts of the database. Finally, if the network data directory is partitioned, then the NDBMS functions that use it must be more complicated.

A point should be made about the centralization alternative. The centralization decision involves a specific component and where to place it. In principle, different components could be centralized at different nodes. Therefore, when discussing the centralized alternative, the particular component should always be specified. For example, one could distribute the database, its definition, and the various DBMS and NDBMS functions, but centralize the network data directory and the network description. One node could be the central node for the directory, whereas the network description could be centralized at another node.

5-4. Summary

This chapter has discussed the basic concepts of a DDBMS. First, it described the components of a DDBMS. It then discussed and evaluated the various distribution alternatives. Finally, it described the way in which the placement decisions for different components are related. The next two chapters provide a more detailed discussion of data and function distribution.

6

Data Distribution

This chapter discusses data distribution: the placement of data within a distributed system. How to distribute the database is one of the four major issues in DDBMS design. (The other three are function distribution, update synchronization, and request decomposition.) For the database administrator (DBA), data distribution is probably the most important area because it is one of the few decisions over which he or she has direct control. Function distribution, update synchronization, and request decomposition decisions will probably be an integral part of the DDBMS design and therefore will be out of the control of the DBA, although he may be able to select a few options in the function distribution area.

Data placement alternatives add another layer of complexity to database design. Although there has been much research on various aspects of the data placement problem, there are currently no good data placement algorithms that consider all the effects of a design alternative.

This chapter consists of three sections, the first of which discusses the basic data distribution concepts. It identifies four criteria for evaluating and comparing various distribution alternatives. It then identifies four distribution alternatives and discusses them in terms of these criteria. The second section reviews some of the main research on data distribution and provides an indication of the state of the art. The third section discusses some of the remaining issues that need to be resolved before a more complete data placement algorithm can be developed.

6–1. Data Placement Alternatives

There are three basic data placement alternatives: centralized, replicated, and partitioned. Replication means that there is a complete copy of the database at every node in the network. With the pure partitioning approach the database is divided into nonoverlapping segments, each of which is placed at a different node. Replication involves many copies of the database, whereas both the centralized and the partitioned approaches allow only a single copy. There are also a variety of hybrid approaches, wherein different methods are used to place different parts of the database. Each of these is discussed in more detail later in this section. First, however, the criteria against which these alternatives are to be measured must be defined.

There are four criteria against which to evaluate each of the four placement alternatives: storage costs, reliability, retrieval costs, and update costs. Each of these criteria will be discussed in more detail. Then each of the placement alternatives is considered in terms of these evaluation criteria.

There are several basic trade-offs among these criteria, principally between storage costs and reliability and between retrieval and update costs. Storage costs are minimized when there is only one copy of the data. The trade-off is that any approach that involves only one copy of the data, although it minimizes storage costs, provides relatively poor reliability for a distributed system. If a node fails, then the part of the database stored at that node is unavailable to all the nodes in the network. In a centralized DBMS, reliability is sometimes used to refer to the backup and recovery capability to recover from damage to or destruction of the database. While the recovery procedures are being peformed, the database is not available to the users, even though the database is only temporarily damaged. In a distributed system, however, reliability is more concerned with the continuous availability of the database. If the database, or the copy of it at a particular node, is damaged, the users should still be able to continue processing with another copy of the database during the recovery procedure. A DDBMS is more reliable if it can continue to operate and make the data available to the users when more components, either nodes or communications links, fail. It would also be considered more reliable if the period during which the data were unavailable was shorter. Therefore, a DDBMS is more reliable if there are more copies of the database. Given the same number of copies, a DDBMS would be considered more reliable if faster recovery were possible. Either of these approaches (that is, more copies or faster recovery) requires additional storage capacity, either for additional copies of the database or for additional backup data so that the recovery can be done faster.

The second major trade-off is between retrieval and update costs. Retrieval costs and time are minimized whenever the use of the communications system is minimized. This leads to multiple copies of the data. In the extreme case the database is replicated, with each node having a complete copy of all the data. In this case every retrieval can be done very cheaply as a local request, with no need to use the communications system. The trade-off here is that although additional copies of the data drive down the retrieval costs, they increase the updating costs. Update synchronization (see chapter 8) is one of the most difficult problems in distributed database, and improvements in the retrieval area seriously complicate this aspect of the system. It is difficult, however, to make general statements about this type of trade-off. Trade-offs between retrieval and update costs are very dependent on the specific patterns of data usage. Therefore, in this trade-off two decisions actually must be made, although they may—indeed probably will—be made jointly. First, there is the decision of what type of data distribution alternative to use. If the partitioned or hybrid approach is selected, then there is a second level of decision, to decide exactly what data to place where. Much of the research reviewed in the next section concerns this detailed design issue of where to place what data. The caveat is that most of these studies were made in a file rather than a database environment.

The rest of this section discusses the various placement alternatives in terms of the foregoing criteria.

Centralized

With the centralized approach, the entire database is stored at a single node. This used to be the only approach, but is now only one of several possible approaches in a distributed system. Because there is only one copy of the database, centralization minimizes storage costs. However, there is a serious problem: single failure of either the hardware or the database can result in a catastrophic failure of the system. For remote users, who must use an expensive communications system, retrieval costs are very high. These retrievals are expensive in terms of both communications costs and time delays. On the other hand, updates are relatively cheap. A single copy of the data eliminates the need for time-consuming and expensive update synchronization algorithms. These synchronization methods require extensive communications and are, therefore, even more expensive than remote retrievals. A final benefit of centralized data placement is that any query that can be expressed in the query language can be processed. With the partitioned and hybrid alternatives, relatively simple changes in the way the data are placed can make some queries unacceptable to some systems.

Replication

Replication involves storing a complete copy of the database at every node in the system, an approach that obviously has the greatest storage costs. The major benefit of this approach is very high reliability, which is one of the basic advantages of any distributed system. If one node fails, the others can continue to operate. This improved reliability is, however, an illusion if the only copy of the data the application needs is stored at the failed node. Replication of the database eliminates this difficulty. As long as any node is available, the entire database is available.

The retrieval cost is very low because almost all retrieval requests can be satisfied locally, without the use of the communications system. However, there are two special cases in which communications does become a factor. Both of these cases arise when another node has made a request to update the data that the local node needs to retrieve. In the first case, where a centralized synchronization technique is used, a query must be sent to a specific node (the primary or dominant node for that data) to guarantee that it obtains the latest version of the data. Otherwise, an update may have been entered and be working its way through the network, but simply not yet have reached the node at which the query request was made. The other situation arises when global locking is used. In this case the data may have been locked by an update request at another node. Although in this case the retrieval request does not need to use the communications system directly, it is affected by the communications system because it cannot be completed until the update is finished and the lock released.

Updates are very expensive in a replicated system because of the synchronization overhead. The complexity of the synchronization procedures and the amount of communications they require are directly dependent on the number of copies. The amount of communications required increases very rapidly as the number of copies increases.

Partitioned

If there is high locality of reference—that is, if most of the requests for certain data come from a specific node—then the database can be partitioned into nonoverlapping segments. Since there is only a single copy of the data, partitioning, like centralization, minimizes storage costs. In both cases, because there is only one copy of the data, there is a reliability problem. If the single copy of the data needed by an application is lost, then for that application, the system is down, even if the hardware is still available. The partitioning approach does have one reliability advantage over the centralized system, however. In the centralized case, if the database node fails, all the data are lost and all the applications are stopped. In the partitioned system, however, only those applications that need the data at the failed node are blocked. Any request that does not need data from the failed node can still be processed. Thus, although a partitioned system still has reliability problems, it is more reliable than a centralized system.

Locality of reference also reduces the overall retrieval cost of the system. Most of the requests can be processed locally and avoid the communications system. Only a request that needs data from another node must pay a performance and cost penalty for communications. In most cases, updates are also cheaper and faster because, since there are no multiple copies to be synchronized, updating only requires locking at a single node. The exception occurs when the update involves data at several nodes, in which case locking across several nodes is required.

Hybrid

Any number of hybrid placement alternatives are possible because different parts of the database can be placed using different methods. For example, one file may be frequently used for retrieval by all or most of the nodes. A copy of this file would then be placed at all the nodes that use it. Another part of the database may be partitioned because it shows a high locality of reference. A basic finding of some of the earlier placement studies was that the number of copies of data in the system should depend on the relative frequency of updates versus retrievals. Only specific hybrid alternatives can be evaluated against the four criteria. Very little can be said to evaluate the hybrid approach in general.

Fragments

Given the distribution alternatives described previoulsy, the concept of a fragment provides a mechanism to specify how to place particular parts of the database. This concept is used for the partitioned and hybrid distribution alternatives. Since the centralized and replicated approaches do not require dividing the database, the concept of a fragment is not necessary for them.

Fragments involve both a logical and a physical concept. A *logical fragment* is a block of data to be placed somewhere in the distributed system. A logical fragment can be described in relational terms as the result of a selection and a projection of the database. In other words, logical fragments can be the result of data-item partitioning, data-value partitioning, or both. Although logical fragments can be defined arbitrarily, collectively they are related because they form disjoint or nonoverlapping subsets of the database. Once the database has been divided into a set of fragments, all the data are in one and only one logical fragment. If one of these logical fragments is stored at a node, it creates a *physical* or *stored fragment*. Each of the logical fragments is placed at one or more nodes depending on which distribution approach is being used. In other words, each logical fragment results in one or more physical fragments depending on the number of copies that are made. If the database is being partitioned, then each logical fragment is placed at one and only one node, so each logical fragment creates only one corresponding stored or physical fragment. If the hybrid distribution approach is being used, then there will be multiple copies of some of the logical fragments—that is, two or more stored fragments.

In addition to providing a conceptual way in which to divide the database, the logical fragment also can be the unit of data to which the network data directory can point. As the next section shows, in much of the earlier data placement work, the logical fragment was simply a file.

6–2. Survey of Previous Research

There has been much previous work on data placement. Most of the earlier studies made a number of assumptions that anyone using their methods must understand. Some of these assumptions related to the type of distributed system that was being analyzed. In other cases simplifying assumptions had to be made before the problem could be solved. Also, much of this research was done for file systems before there was a full understanding of the problems of synchronizing updates in a distributed database. An example of this type of problem occurred in one of Chu's early studies in the way he defined the cost of an update when there are replicated copies of the data.[1] He assumed that the update costs were the communications costs of sending the update request to every node that had a copy of the data. In a file system, where the entire file could be locked before the program began, this was a reasonable approximation. In a distributed database with multiple users at many nodes, however, this is not sufficient for update synchronization. For example, one relatively simple synchronization approach (global locking) actually requires five messages for each copy, not including any redundant messages for improved reliability and fault tolerance. An acceptable model must include both the actual update message and all the control and acknowledgment messages required for both synchronization and reliability. The important point is that although Chu's approach was acceptable for the file systems with which he was concerned, significant changes are necessary if this analysis method is to be used in a distributed database environment. Similarly, all these early placement models must be modified and updated to include valid synchronization and reliability algorithms. The results of much of the more recent synchronization research must be factored into these earlier placement studies to make them appropriate for DDBMSs.

The purpose of this section is to review and explain this earlier data placement research. This includes an explanation of the models, the assumptions underlying them, and the problems with these approaches. The last section then discusses some of the issues that must be addressed to update this work and make it useful for the system designer and the database administrator, who must decide how to place the data in a DDBMS.

One of the basic, early file placement studies was done by Chu in 1969.[2] By making certain assumptions and imposing certain constraints, he reduced the placement decision to a linear integer programming problem. This section initially describes Chu's work and then shows how it has been extended by subsequent research. The purpose of Chu's study was to determine the optimal placement of files within a distributed system. The objective function was to minimize the system operating costs, including both storage and communications costs. The constraints he imposed were the storage capacities for each node and the maximum allowable access time for each file at each node. The following variables were included in the model:

1. storage costs
2. storage capacity at each node
3. communications costs
4. retrieval rate for each file at each node
5. update rate for each file at each node
6. maximum allowable access time at each node for each file

The storage costs are specified in a cost matrix: $C(i,j)$. This matrix specifies the unit costs of storing file j at node i. Therefore, the actual costs for storing the file are this unit cost times the length of the file. Although it is not used in Chu's analysis, this approach would permit different types of storage devices to be specified for different files. Some files could be stored in an archival storage, whereas other, more active files could be stored on faster, more expensive devices. A storage-capacity constraint is also placed on each node. A three-dimensional matrix is used to define the communications costs. This matrix, $A(i,j,k)$, specifies the unit costs of tranferring file j from node k to node i. This unit cost must also be multiplied by the file length to obtain the total communications costs. More than just the communications costs can be built into this cost matrix. This matrix can include the costs for processing the query at node i, the communications cost for sending the query to node k, the processing cost at node k, the communications cost for returning file j to node i, and the subsequent processing cost at node i. Implicit in the use of this type of cost matrix is that there is only one request processing strategy. Different strategies would result in different costs, and this algorithm has no way of dealing with different cost matrixes. A similar matrix and set of equations are defined for communication times. Instead of unit cost, this matrix has the unit of time required to transmit a block of data over the path. This time matrix, in effect, defines the bandwidth of the various paths linking the nodes. There is also a matrix specifying the expected retrieval and update rates for each file by each node. Finally, there is a constraint that specifies the maximum time for which each node can wait for each file. Although it is not done, the analysis could be generalized to allow a different maximum response time for retrievals and updates.

As originally defined, this file placement problem was a nonlinear integer programming problem. It is then reduced to a more manageable linear integer programming problem by making a number of assumptions. First, Chu assumes that the communications system and the node configuration—that is, storage capacities—are given. This includes the topology of node connections, the bandwidth of each path, and the unit costs of sending messages between each set of nodes. This definitely requires static message routing, which in turn affects system reliability.

A second assumption involves the complexity of the paths between nodes. Although it is not stated, the model requires a direct connection between any two nodes that communicate with each other.

Third, Chu assumes that the time delay is entirely in the communication system—that is, that the time required to retrieve a file at a node where it is stored is insignificant.

Fourth, he assumes that request messages are shorter than responses and, therefore, should have a higher priority in the communications system. This is still a reasonable assumption.

Finally, there are two assumptions about the retrieval and update operations. Only one copy of the file (or part of the file) needs to be accessed for a retrieval. If the file is not at the requesting node, then it can be obtained from any node that has a copy, as long as the specified time constraint can be met. For updates, a single request message needs to be sent to every node that stores a copy of the file.

These assumptions are reconsidered and in some cases relaxed in later studies, which will be reviewed. However, the critical assumptions minimizing the update complexity have not yet been adequately addressed.

Whitney relaxed some of Chu's assumptions and considered a more complex problem.[3] If the objective is to minimize operating costs, then why should the analysis start with a given communication system, which itself may be a major cost factor? Whitney started with a set of nodes and a set of files and jointly solved two problems—how to place the files and how to connect the nodes. In effect, he integrated the file placement problem with the design of the communications system. However, he did assume given node storage capacities.

Like Chu and Whitney, Mahmoud and Riordon were concerned with optimal file placement.[4] They also assumed a specific network (that is, a defined topology, bandwidths for each link, and a specified set of communications costs); but they then define a slightly different problem. The objective is still to minimize the operating costs. However, like Whitney, they consider a joint set of decisions to be made. One set of decisions concerns file placement in a given network. The difference is that the storage allocation at each node is no longer fixed. In addition to determining the optimal file placement, the analysis also determines the optimal way in which to allocate storage capacity among the nodes. Constraints are imposed based on delays within the communications system and the availability of the file when it is needed. As with Chu's original model, this results in a nonlinear integer programming problem. Unfortunately, such problems are computationally intractable. Whereas Chu chose to add additional constraints to create linearity, Mahmoud and Riordon chose to accept the nonlinearity and develop a heuristic algorithm, thereby reducing the computational complexity of the problem.

The algorithm initially determines the minimum number of copies of files necessary to satisfy the availability constraint. It then determines the set of possible solutions using this distribution. Next, it attempts to improve on this distribution by adding and deleting copies of files, subject to a number of explicit decision rules. The iterations are stopped when several iterations fail to provide any improvement. This method can only provide very good solutions, not optimal ones. The trade-off, however, is that the processing time for the analysis may be reduced by as much as an order of magnitude. An additional problem is that this approach finds only a local—not the global—optimum.

Levin and Morgan extended the previous work in two ways.[5] First, they made a distinction between programs and data. Their point was that data could be sent to the requesting node and processed, or, conversely, the program could be sent to the node with the data and the request processed there. Because program conversion is a difficult process in a heterogeneous system, in most cases the data rather than the programs are transmitted. However, this distinction did not create a problem because one of the first assumptions in Levin's dissertation was that the network consists of homogeneous nodes. Even if this were not the case, the heterogenity is less severe in a DDBMS because in most cases the "program" is simply a high-level data management request, the translation of which is much less difficult than automatic program conversion.

Levin and Morgan's second contribution, which does directly relate to the data placement problem, was to recognize three distinct types of placement problems. First, there is the type of problem that Chu and the others considered—static file assignment given complete information. In this case, the pattern of file access is known and does not change.

The second type of problem involves a dynamic pattern of access, but, again, with complete information. In this case the pattern of access changes. For example, the database is used in one way at the first of the month, in a second way during the month, and in yet a third pattern during month-end processing. This forces the analyst to select one of two options. One approach is to select an "average" pattern of use and optimize the placement as if the file access were static with this average behavior. The other approach is to determine an optimum placement for each pattern of usage and select conversion points at which the files are shifted from one location to another. In other words, a trade-off is made to determine when the overhead of shifting from one placement alternative to another balances the inefficiencies of using a nonoptimal placement after the changed pattern of use. In reality, the shift may not be directly from one optimal to another. The complete change may be made in a series of steps as the access pattern gradually changes. Although this problem is more complicated, it is still relatively manageable because it assumes complete information about how the file is used.

The third type of problem arises when the assumption of complete information is removed. In this case, the designer does not know a priori what the access pattern or patterns are. Some type of system monitoring is necessary to determine this. Once the system has been sufficiently monitored, then the pattern or patterns of access are known and the problem reduces to one of the aforementioned two—a static or a dynamic pattern of access.

Akoka and Chen have provided perhaps the most complete model to date.[6] It considers simultaneously the distribution of the data, the programs, the processing power, and the communications network. The model attempts to optimize the cost of the overall system. To do this, it considers the costs of the computers, the communications lines, and the storage requirements for both the database and the programs. It also considers the communications costs for both queries and updates in two stages. The first stage is the communications cost from the node where the request enters the system to the node where the necessary programs are stored. The second stage is the communications costs from the node where the programs are stored to the node where the necessary part of the database is stored. Their objective function considers each of these types of cost. The constraints involve the processing power, transaction routes, and residency of various databases and programs. First, the processing power of a node must not be exceeded by the processing requirements of the transactions that are processed there. Second, there must be a communications path so that every transaction can be routed to the necessary nodes and programs. Finally, databases and programs must be assigned to nodes in a way that is consistent with the previously defined routings.

Since their model results in a nonlinear integer programming problem, its solution is normally very difficult. However, Akoka and Chen developed a "bounded branch and bound" solution algorithm that quickly converges to a "good" solution, although not necessarily the optimal solution.

Most of these analyses, especially the earlier ones, have problems that prevent them from being used as distributed database design tools. The next section discusses some issues that must be resolved in order to develop these design tools.

6–3. Future Research

Past research in data placement issues has addressed specific parts of the problem one at a time. Related issues such as update synchronization and request decomposition were not explicitly included. For a given type of transaction, the necessary processing was described explicitly. *Implicit* in this description was a set of synchronization procedures and decomposition rules. In order to do a sensitivity analysis to determine how different rules and procedures would affect the performance of a particular data distribution alternative, the database designer had to redefine manually all the transactions and how they would be performed. This type of manual modification was also required in some cases to evaluate different placement alternatives. As a mimimum, there must be a much more user-friendly front-end interface for these design routines. Most of these routines have not yet been developed to the point at which they could really be considered design tools. These design tools must be developed, however, because of the complexity of developing a DDBMS. They are also needed by the DBA simply to design a distributed database, even when he is given an operational DDBMS. These tools are also necessary because human intuition is not very good with very complex systems. What may appear to be relatively simple design changes may result in drastic performance differences.

Two types of tools are necessary because there are two distinct objectives. One of these is to be able to analyze many alternatives relatively quickly and cheaply. This is necessary to narrow the many possibilities down to a few promising alternatives. The important factor here is the high speed and low cost of the solutions, even if the results are only approximations. The second objective is to do a much more detailed and, therefore, more expensive analysis of those selected few alternatives. Problem statements that permit analytical solutions are more appropriate for the former case, whereas simulation methods are more appropriate in the latter.

Analytical tools have three major benefits. First, they are simpler and easier to formulate, in part because they frequently involve simplifying assumptions. Second, they tend to be faster and easier to solve, again with the appropriate simplifying assumptions. Analytical tools allow far more alternatives to be evaluated because solving each one is relatively cheap. By considering a variety of approaches, the analyst can frequently develop a better insight into the specific problem. This also allows the analyst to identify and focus on a few specific solutions that seem to offer the most promise. These solutions can then be analyzed in more detail, usually with simulation tools.

Analytical methods do have three potential problems. First, the simplifying assumptions required to define and solve the analytical model may not be realistic. To determine whether or not this is the case, the analyst must know the assumptions (such as the implied statistical distribution or linearity) implicit in the analytical mode, and how well these assumptions apply in the specific real case. If the assumptions hold, then obviously the method can be used. If the assumptions are not appropriate in the specific case, then the analyst must determine how much they are violated and evaluate the consequences. The effects on the solution may be minor enough that the results are still acceptable, especially if later, more detailed simulation methods are going to be used.

Second, analytical methods provide only the average performance of the system. They do not provide more complete information, such as standard deviations and sensitivity analysis. Finally, it is difficult to study the effects of failure on the system. For example, knowing that a resource is not available 10 percent of the time is not the same as simply reducing its overall capacity by 10 percent. The effects of a failure or a lack of availability at certain points can have serious consequences that ripple through various parts of the system. In summary, analytical tools can be very effective for studying the overall performance of the system, for analyzing relatively small pieces of the system, and for quickly and cheaply evaluating many alternatives. They are less useful for analyzing the detailed performance of relatively large, complex systems.

Simulation methods are more appropriate for these types of problems. One of the major problems with simulations is that they can be very expensive. This is especially true when one remembers that a single simulation run, which may have been relatively lengthy, is simply one experiment. A significant number of runs must be made just to be able to infer anything about even one configuration. Therefore, considering very many alternatives or configurations very drastically increases the costs of the analysis. This is why analytical models are necessary to narrow down the focus of the simulation studies.

The high costs of simulation studies are justified because of flexibility of such studies. The simulation model can define the actual step-by-step procedures that the DDBMS will use. This procedural definition can be done at any level of detail, with different parts of the system being simulated in different levels of detail. Furthermore, although an analytical model is predicated on one of a few specific types of statistical distribution, a simulation model can be used in any distribution for such random occurrences as the arrival of transactions at a node. In fact, one could monitor an existing system and use the actual arrival pattern in a simulation analysis. This capability, along with the step-by-step procedural definition of the model, allows a much more complete analysis of the effects of a failure in the system. For certain types of distributed system, this analysis is very important because fault tolerance may have been one of the main reasons for selecting a distributed system. Finally, because a simulation run usually provides a detailed log of all the events, much more analysis can be done of any aspect of the system's performance.

In summary, distributed database management systems cannot be developed or used effectively without much better design tools, such as the analytical and simulation approaches described in this chapter.

Notes

1. W.W. Chu, "Optimal File Allocation in a Multiple Computer System," *IEEE Trans. on Computers* 18, no. 10 (October 1969):885–889.

2. Ibid.

3. V.K.M. Whitney, *A Study of Optimal File Assignment and Communication Network Configuration* (Ph.D. Diss. University of Michigan, 1970).

4. S. Mahmoud and J.S. Riordon, "Optimal Allocation of Resources in Distributed Information Networks," *ACM Trans. on Database Systems* 1, no. 1 (March 1976):66–78.

5. K.D. Levin and H.L. Morgan, "Optimizing Distributed Data Bases— A Framework for Research," *Proc. NCC 1975*, pp. 473–478.

6. J. Akoka and P.P.S. Chen, "Optimization of Distributed Database Systems and Computer Networks," Center for Information Systems Research, Massachusetts Institute of Technology, WP 916–77 (March 1977).

7 Function Distribution

Chapter 6 discussed the placement of the data. This chapter focuses on the second, often ignored, distribution issue—how to distribute the functions of a distributed database management system (DDBMS). Most of the work in the distributed database area assumes that there is a complete DDBMS with all the functions at every node. This probably will not be the case in a heterogeneous system, however, especially where there are major differences in the capability of various nodes, which may be large mainframes, minicomputers, or microcomputers. The distribution decision considered in this chapter involves the placement of the system-level data management functions. These functions are clustered together to build the user-level functions, such as retrieve, modify, add, and delete.

This chapter is organized into two main sections, the first of which describes and explains the various steps in processing a request. These steps are the functions or procedures that can be distributed. Some of them are traditional data management functions that would be performed by the local DBMS. Others are NDBMS functions, which are required only because of the distributed environment. (Some of the literature uses the terms *local* and *global data managers* for the DBMS and the NDBMS.) Although some of the NDBMS functions would be performed differently depending on how updates are synchronized and how requests are decomposed, this chapter concentrates on the generic functions. The details of update synchronization and request decomposition are left for the next two chapters. The system architect specifies which functions are clustered at a node. The second section of the chapter identifies some of the ways these functions can be clustered.

7–1. Distributed Database Management Functions

Chapter 2 described the functions of a centralized DBMS. This section provides a comparable list of functions for a distributed database management system. A complete node has all of these functions. A range of configurations is possible by adding functions to a set of minimal node types, which is described in the next section. Once the set of DDBMS functions has been identified, the next question is how to distribute the functions. Therefore, specific distribution alternatives are described in the next section on node configurations.

The function list discussed later was derived by identifying the processing steps for a compound retrieval request. Although there is some general discussion of the additional functions required to synchronization updates, a detailed discussion of these functions is deferred until chapter 8. Duplicate functions such as the communications functions involved in transmitting a request and later the response, are not repeated in the list. Later, in discussing specific distribution alternatives, the functions are listed in the exact sequence in which they occur; so, when appropriate, a function is repeated in these lists.

The functions are listed as follows.[1] A separate discussion of each function follows the list. The functions include:

1. Accept the user's request.
2. Check the request for validity.
3. Check the user's authorization.
4. Translate the request.
5. Determine a network-wide request processing strategy.
6. Encrypt the request.
7. Determine the routing.
8. Transmit the request through the communications system.
9. Decrypt the request.
10. Determine the local processing strategy.
11. Locate the data in the logical data structure.
12. Locate the data in the physical data structure.
13. Do the physical I/O.
14. Convert the data to the form expected by the user.
15. Translate the data.
16. Return the response to the requesting node.
17. Consolidate, sort, edit, and format the response.
18. Display the response to the user.

Accept the User's Request

At this point the network database management system (NDBMS) simply accepts the request from the user. The request may be a low-level one for a single record; ideally, however, it would be a high-level, nonprocedural one, so that the NDBMS could determine how to optimize it. The request may be for local data or for data stored at another node. The NDBMS eventually determines whether the request is local or requires data from another node. It then passes the request to either the local DBMS or the communications software. This decision is made at a later step in the process, however. In some cases the original user request may cause the NDBMS to generate many subrequests, but this decomposition also occurs at a later step. At this point it is also irrelevant whether the request is for retrieval or update.

Check the Request for Validity

This function edits the request and attempts to detect any errors. The first check is to ensure that the request conforms to the syntax and format of the query language. Further checks are required to ensure that the record and field types specified actually exist. This check requires the subschema (or the external schema of the three-level database architecture is being used). If the subschema is not stored at the node where the request is entered, then this check cannot be made until the request has been forwarded to another node that does contain the subschema.

Check the User's Authorization

If the request is valid, the next step is to determine whether the user has the authority to access the data and to perform the specified operations on it. This function requires that part of the schema with the access control information. Therefore, it is possible that this check cannot be done at the requesting node but must be deferred until the request has been transmitted to another node that does contain the necessary part of the schema. In fact, access control and security checks could be spread over several nodes. How much security is provided depends on the specific DDBMS. As a minimum, many current centralized DBMSs control user access by the operation requested and the record types and fields being used. If possible, both of these types of checks should be made at this point. Content-based security, which depends on the value stored in a record, cannot be checked at this point. This type of check must be deferred until the data have been retrieved. As a general rule, access control and security checks should be made as soon as possible. Moreover, in a very secure system these checks may be repeated several times. For example, the request is entered at one node, and its authorizations are checked before it is forwarded to the node that has the data. The node with the data now has two options. It can automatically accept the request as authorized, assuming that the originating node would have blocked any unauthorized requests. The more secure approach, however, is for every node to verify the authorization of any request it processes. This requires that the access control information be replicated at all the data nodes. Although repeating these authorization checks is more time consuming and expensive, it provides a much greater level of security.

Translate the Request

This function, required only in a heterogeneous system, translates requests from one type of DBMS to another. Ideally, the placement of data and the hardware and software (DBMS) under which they are stored should be transparent to the user. This function provides this hardware and DBMS independence by doing any necessary translation of the request. This translation could be required at two levels. At one level only the hardware is different. The same DBMS is used at both the requesting and the data nodes. At another level different types of DBMSs may be involved. For example, a CODASYL-type request may be issued for data stored in a relational database. As was shown in chapter 2 in the section on the common data model, in principle this type of translation can be handled. In general, three translation possibilities exist, as shown in figure 7–1. In practice, generalized translation can be very difficult. Therefore, in many cases homongeneous systems will be used to eliminate the need for this translation function.

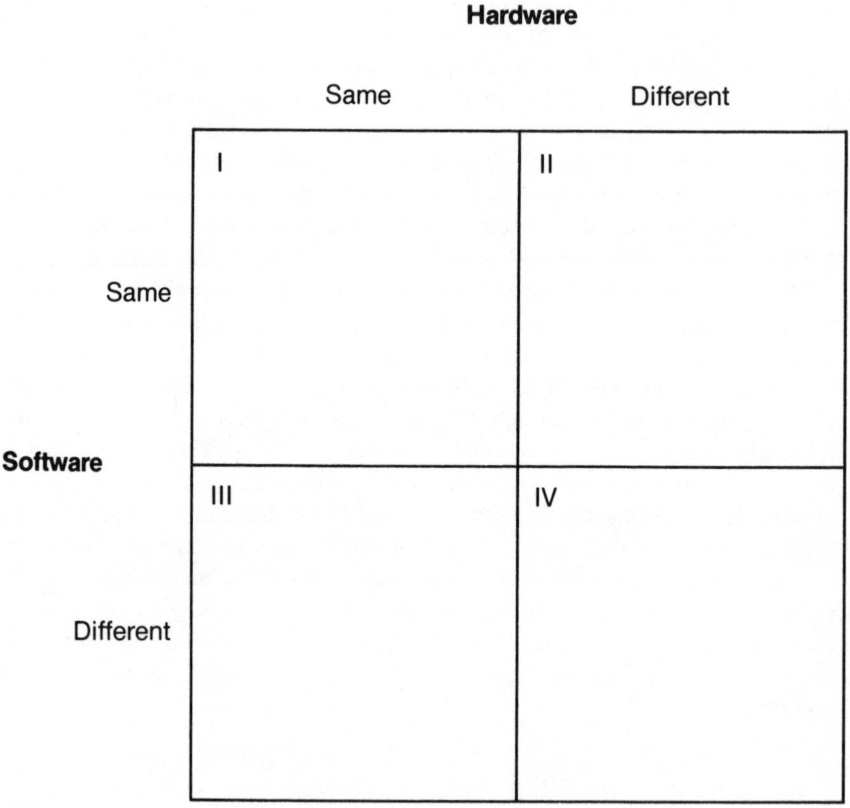

Hardware

	Same	Different
Same	I	II
Different	III	IV

Software

Figure 7–1. Translation Alternatives

A related function may be required later to translate the data response from one type of DBMS to another. This function is discussed in step 15.

Determine a Network-wide Request Processing Strategy

This can be the most complex of the new functions required by the NDBMS. The degree of complexity depends on the flexibility provided by the NDBMS. If the specific system design allows only local and remote requests, then this function is relatively simple. All it needs to do is determine the node to which to send the request.

Compound requests require processing by several nodes. For these requests there are two closely related parts to this function. First, the function must determine how to process and coordinate the request. This involves query or request decomposition, which is discussed in more detail in chapter 9. The second part of the function is the same as for remote request—to determine the node to which to send the request. The only difference is that by this point the original request may have been decomposed into many subrequests, and a destination node must be determined for each of them. The problem is that these two decisions are interdependent and must be made jointly, not sequentially.

Several things must be done for query decomposition. First, the network data directory, assuming there is one, is used to determine the alternative nodes that can do part of the processing. For example, in a relational system the NDBMS must determine which relations are needed to process the request and which, if any, must be joined. The next step is to identify the nodes at which these relations are stored. This list of nodes then allows the NDBMS to determine the possible ways in which the request could be processed. Then, using a request decomposition algorithm, one of the alternatives is selected. If a procedural query language is used, the user must specify which relations to use and how they are joined. This simplifies the query decomposition by forcing the user to do more of the work. If a nonprocedural language is used, then the NDBMS must use the schema to determine which relations to use and how to join them to create the necessary access paths. A similar sequence of steps must be applied in a distributed CODASYL database. The NDBMS must determine which record types or sets are needed and where they are stored. Depending on whether a low- or high-level query language is used, the NDBMS must do more or less work to identify the alternative ways of processing the request. Finally, once an alternative is selected, the NDBMS uses the network data directory to identify the nodes to which the request or subrequests should be sent.

In some cases there is only one node that can process the request; but in other cases any one of several nodes may be able to satisfy the request. When the system is designed, a procedure must be developed to determine to which node the request should be sent. One node is usually selected from all those that qualify, and the request is only sent there. (An alternate design could broadcast the request to all the nodes that could process it and accept the first response. However, this approach would not be used except in special systems because it would result in redundant communications and processing.) The single destination node could be selected either at this point as part of the strategy selection or later in the communications software as part of the routing procedure. If the selection is made at this point, the request and a single node identifier are sent to the routing function. In this case, the decision could be defined statically at system design time. For example, each node could have a prioritized list of nodes with which it could communicate. Whenever a request could be sent to any one of several nodes, a simple algorithm could select the node highest on the priority list. This method could even provide some load balancing because every node does not have to have the same priority list.

The other approach is to pass all the alternate node identifiers to the routing procedure and allow it to select the best node, depending on the current load on the communications system. However, attempting to optimize at this point would seriously complicate the routing algorithm, and the performance improvement might not be worth the extra effort.

In some networks, the node identification may be a trivial or nonexistent function. Some networks, especially local loop architectures, may not use a network data directory. Since every request is routed through every node in a ring, each node could check the request against a local directory to see whether it had the data and could process the request. However, a network or global directory could still be used in this case. If it were, the logical node identifier would be prefixed to the request. Then only the node that was addressed would actually have to process the request.

Encrypt the Request

This function may or may not be provided, depending on the level of security required by the system. If it is provided, at this point the request is encrypted prior to being passed to the communications subsystem. The request is encrypted, transmitted through the communications system, and decrypted at the destination mode. The request must be decrypted at the destination node before it can be interpreted and processed. Therefore, encryption only provides communications security. This function is different from the current one provided by some DBMSs, which actually encrypt the data before it is stored on the database. The most secure system would use both types of encryption.

The basic function is to encrypt a message before it is sent to the communications software. The same function would be provided at the data node to encrypt the response before returning it to the requesting node. It is irrelevant to the encryption/decryption procedures whether the message to be processed is a request or a data response.

Determine the Routing

This function converts a logical node identifier into a physical node address and does the routing to determine the path over which the request should be sent. It uses the logical node identifier and the network description to determine the paths over which to send the request or the response. The path may be directly from the source to the destination node or may pass through several intermediate nodes. If intermediate nodes are allowed, then there is a second design choice. The full route may be determined initially and the intermediate nodes simply pass the message on to the next predetermined node. Alternatively, each node can determine only the routing to the next node. Each node then determines the next node to which to pass the message so that it will ultimately get to its destination. If this approach is used, some checks must be made to ensure that a message does not get trapped in a loop and fail to be delivered. The routing decision can be made statically when the system is designed or dynamically for each request. In fact, with packet switching a routing decision is made for each packet in the message.

Normally, the routing procedure is given a single logical node identifier. Additional flexibility could be provided by allowing the routing procedure to accept multiple logical node identifiers. This flexibility could be used in two cases. In the first case the message could be broadcast to all the specified nodes. In the second case the message would need to be sent only to one of the nodes. Since any node could satisfy the request, the routing procedure could select the one that should provide the fastest response. The trade-off is that at some point the optimizing algorithm becomes more complex and time consuming than its savings justify.

The routing function is the same regardless of whether a request or a data response is involved, although there are significant differences in how the logical node identifier is determined. A response is simply returned to the requesting node or to an alternate destination node that was specified in the request. A request, however, can require a relatively complex NDBMS function to determine its destination node.

Transmit the Request through the Communications System

At this point a message (either a request or a response), which may or may not be encrypted, is passed to the communications software for delivery to its destination. The function of the various layers in the communications system are discussed in chapter 3, and there is nothing unique about them when they are used in conjunction with a DDBMS. The messages are passed down through the communications layers at the source node, transmitted to the destination, and passed up through the corresponding layers at the destination node.

Decrypt the Request

If the request has been encrypted at the source node, then this is the point at which it would be decrypted at the destination node before being processed.

Determine the Local Processing Strategy

At this point the request is now at the NDBMS of the node that has the necessary data and can process it. If the request was an update, this is the point at which the NDBMS would do the necessary synchronization. The request is then passed to the local DBMS for processing. Although this request may actually be only one of many subrequests into which the user's original request was decomposed, once it reaches this point, the local DBMS can process it as if it were a local request. The local DBMS is very much like current centralized DBMSs.

This strategy selection is the first of four basic functions that the local DBMS must perform. At this point it must select a strategy for processing the request locally. Primarily, this involves determining which access paths to use. There is a fuzzy boundary between this function and the next two. All three functions must be performed, but they are so interrelated that making a clear distinction between them is difficult unless a specific implementation is being discussed.

Locate the Data in the Logical Data Structure

To perform this function, the local DBMS must have the request, the user's subschema (the external schema in the three-level architecture), and the logical part of the schema (the conceptual schema). This allows the DBMS to do the necessary mapping between the user's view of the data and the logical structure of the local part of the database.

Locate the Data in the Physical Data Structure

The local DBMS now takes the results of the previous step and maps them into the physical structure of the database. This means determining the device or devices on which the requested data are stored and the location of these devices. This is done using the results of the previous logical mapping and the physical definition part of the schema (the internal schema in the three-level architecture). Specifically, this may mean simply mapping record identifiers into physical address. Since the user's view of the data should be independent of their physical location, the subschema is not needed for this step.

If the request had been an update instead of a retrieval, this would be the last point at which the data could have been locked. However, the data may have been locked before this, possibly at the point at which the local processing strategy was being determined. This locking is done by the local DBMS and affects only the local copy of the data. Any synchronization required because of the distributed environment or multiple copies of the data would have been done previously by the NDBMS. Since local requests are passed to the local DBMS through the NDBMS, any conflicts between them and requests originating elsewhere in the network would also have been resolved earlier by the NDBMS.

Do the Physical I/O

This is the point at which the requested data are either read or written. For retrieval the data are simply read into a buffer. For an update this step is more complicated and varies depending on the way the sychronization procedures are implemented. In some implementations the processing would not get to this point unless everything had been synchronized and the update could be committed. In other implementations, the synchronization may not have been ensured, so a flag would be set to indicate that the update had been made logically but had not yet been committed. Only when all the nodes with a copy of the data had gotten to this point would the update actually be committed and written out. Another approach is that the update is actually committed and written at this point but would be backed out if the synchronization procedure fails. The details of various synchronization procedures are discussed in the next chapter.

Convert the Data to the Form Expected by the User

This function requires the data in their stored form, that part of the schema that describes them, and that part of the user's subschema that describes the format in which the user expects the data. This function may be performed at the data node, the requesting node, or any intermediate node as long as the data and all the necessary schema and subschema information are present.

Translate the Data

If the system is heterogeneous, then some additional translation may be necessary between different hardware, different software (DBMSs), or both. This translation function could also be done at any of the three locations (data node, requesting node, or intermediate node) at which the conversion is done. If there are many different types of systems in the network, then this translation may be done in a two-step procedure. At the data node, the data could be translated from the format of the local system into an intermediate network standard format. Then, once the data were returned to the requesting node, they could be translated from the network standard into the local format. If the request involved an update, then the translation could be done in the opposite direction—that is, from the requesting node to the node where the update was to be made.

Return the Response to the Requesting Node

This function is simply the inverse of several of the previous steps. The response, which may or may not be encrypted, is passed through the various communictions layers at both the data and the requesting node and, if necessary, decrypted at the requesting node. Depending on where the conversion and translation functions are done, this communications function may have been done before one or both of them. Although the assumption is that the response is returned to the requesting node, this is not essential. The request could have specified an alternate destination node. The key point is that with a response the destination node is known, so there is not a problem of determining where the response should be sent. This is simpler than the function required to determine where to send the request.

Consolidate, Sort, Edit, and Format the Response

This function involves preparing the response so it can be presented to the user. With a compound request that has been decomposed into several separate requests, there may be multiple responses from various nodes. These responses must then be consolidated into a single response. This function also creates the actual report or screen format requested by the user. Except in the case of a "dumb terminal," this function would probably be done at the requesting node at which the report is to be displayed. This is because formatting is usually data generating. By doing this function at the node at which the data are to be displayed, the amount of data to be transmitted through the system is minimized.

Display the Response to the User

This is simply the function of presenting the requested data to the user. If the request had been an update, this function would display the status of the operation—that is, that the update had been completed or that there were problems that prevented it from being completed.

7–2. Node Configurations

Although many function distribution alternatives are possible, only a few are really practical. This section describes several types of nodes that can be derived by clustering related functions. Some of the minimal node configurations may not be practical, but they provide the basic building blocks from which the system designer can begin. The node types discussed in this section include:

1. minimal user node
2. minimal data node
3. minimal network data directory node
4. minimal network description node
5. database computer node
6. complete node

The minimal nodes have communications software and only one of the following components: a user interface, a part of the database and the minimal supporting DBMS software, the network data directory, or the network description. A minimal user node contains only a user interface and the minimum communications software. It has no data or data management functions. Similarly, a minimal data node contains only data and the minimal data management functions necessary to access them. This type of node contains no user interface or higher-level NDBMS functions. A minimal network data directory node does not contain a user interface or any part of the database or the data management functions. Its sole function is to determine the node or nodes to which a request should be sent. In most cases this node would also route the messages to the proper node. It is possible, however, to isolate the message-routing function at another node. This would be a minimal network description or message-routing node.

These minimal node configurations provide the basic building blocks for the design of a distributed database management system. The system architect can create exactly the type of node that is needed by adding functions to one of these minimal configurations. Two examples included in this section are the database computer node and the complete node. A database computer node has all or part of the database and all the DBMS functions. It may or may not have the NDBMS functions. If there are multiple database computer nodes in the network, each one may have a complete copy the database, or only a part of it. In either case, however, they would all have a complete set of DBMS functions. A complete node contains all the functions described in the previous section.

Direct communications between two nodes may be impossible unless one of them is a complete node. For example, consider a minimal user node and a minimal data node. For communications to occur, there must be a complete set of functions. Collectively, these two minimal node types do not provide a complete set of functions. Therefore, they cannot directly communicate with each other. The missing functions must be provided by one or more intermediate nodes. This difficulty can seriously complicate the systems design. The obvious way to avoid the entire problem is always to use complete nodes, and in many cases this will be done. However, in some heterogeneous networks this may not be possible. Some nodes (for example, microcomputers) may not have sufficient processing power and storage to be complete nodes. In this case this communications problem would arise and would have to be resolved by the system architect.

Even when two nodes, such as two complete nodes, can communicate, a coordination problem can arise. How do the two nodes determine which one does which function? For example, both nodes should not try to decompose the request. This problem is simplified when all the nodes have a complete set of functions. In this case a standard interface can be defined when the system is designed. The functions a node needs to perform would then be independent of the source or destination of the message.

The rest of this section provides a more detailed discussion of each of the node configurations just described.

Minimal User Node

A minimal user node provides only a user interface to the DDBMS. It has no data or data management facilities. Therefore, it must transmit every request to another node. A minimal user node performs only four functions, all of which involve interfaces, two with the user and two with the communications software. First, a minimal user node must be able to accept a request from the user. Second, it must be able to present a message back to the user. Since this type of node does not contain any part of the schema or subschema and can do no data conversion, the message presented to the user is in the same form in which it was received from the communications software. All data conversion must be done at another node that has access to the necessary part of the schema and subschema.

All nodes must have certain minimal communications software to link them into the network. Therefore, the minimal user node has an interface to this software and can pass messages to and from it. These are the other two functions performed by the minimal user node, interface with the communications software. There are a number of specific functions that the communications software must perform. These functions were discussed in chapter 3 in the secton on the ISO seven-level communications architecture. Except for selecting the destination node and routing, these functions are not considered here because they are essentially independent of the type of node. Because a minimal user node does not have a network data directory or a network description, it cannot select a destination node or do routing. Therefore, this type of node must always pass a request to the same destination node over a predefined path. In effect, a minimal user node operates very much like a "dumb terminal."

If additional functions are included, the minimal user node can be enhanced in several ways. If a network description is added, then requests can be routed to different nodes rather than always being sent to the same node. However, unless the node has more information—that is, the network data directory—the user would have to specify the destination node. Therefore, a copy of all or part of the network data directory would be another logical extension. Other enhancements are possible if part of the database definition is stored at the node. The node could do some validity checking if the acceptable record and field names were stored locally. If access control information were stored locally, then authorizations could also be checked. At the other end of the processing, when the response is returned, if more of the schema and subschema were stored locally, then the node could do some of the data conversion and formatting. If all these enhancements are made, then the node is much closer to a complete node than to its original minimal user configuration.

This functional enhancement is the process the system designer must go through to tailor a node to a specific set of requirements. One consideration in the design could be the amount of processing power and storage that are needed and available at a node. Placing a minimal set of functions at a node would minimize the cost of the node. However, it could also necessitate more communications.

Minimal Data Node

A minimal data node must include part of the database, part of the schema describing it, and a subset of the DBMS functions. This subset must be sufficient to retrieve the schema and the data from the database. Additional data management functions could be added to this configuration to permit updates, but this would require adding procedures to control the integrity of the database. All the requests for data must be expressed in terms of the physical aspects of the schema (the internal schema in the three-level database architecture) because this is the only part of the schema stored locally. The data must have been located in the logical data structure before the request was passed to a minimal data node because the local part of the schema does not describe the logical data structure. For example, in the extreme case the node may be given a list of record identifiers. All the node would have to do would be to locate physically the corresponding records, read them, and transmit them back to the request node. All the conversion and mapping would have to be done at another node.

In principle, there can be two types of minimal data nodes, one allowing only retrieval and one also permitting updates. However, the one allowing updates would be far more complex. For retrieval, the minimal data node needs only a small subset of a local DBMS. But for the updates it also needs part of the synchronization procedures from the NDBMS. A minimal data node must be able to perform four functions, two of them involving interfacing with the communications software. That part of the DBMS that is at the node must be able to accept requests from the communications software. It must also be able to pass messages or responses back to the requesting node. The third function is to use the local part of the schema to locate the data physically. Finally, the minimal data node must be able to do the physical I/O. At a minimum this means being able to retrieve the data and the local part of the schema. If the node is for retrieval only, then there must also be a way to load the local part of the database initially. However, this could be done by a load routine, similar to a file copy, rather than by an update of the database. If updates are also permitted at the node, then it must also be able to lock and unlock data and perform any necessary local synchronization procedures. The actual physical locking of the data would have to be performed at this node, although another node may lock the data at a logical level. This logical lock could perhaps simultaneously lock all the copies of the data. Obviously, if the system did not allow replicated data, then the update procedures could be much simpler.

As with the minimal user node, there is a series of enhancements that could be made to a minimal data node. If only retrievals are allowed, then adding the necessary functions to permit updates could be a reasonable first enhancement. Other parts of the schema could be added to allow the node to locate the data in the logical data structure, instead of just in the physical structure. Similarly, if the subschema and the necessary procedures were added, the node could also do some of the conversion of the data before returning it to the user. Again, as these functions are added, the capability of the node becomes more like that of a complete node than of a minimal one.

Minimal Network Data Directory Node

There are two other types of minimal nodes, neither of which has a user interface or any part of the database. One of them is the minimal network data directory node. Because this node has a copy—perhaps the only copy—of the network data directory, it can perform one of the key NDBMS functions: it can take a request and determine the logical identifiers of the nodes that can satisfy it. In its simplest form this node could process only remote requests. In other words, given a request that could be satisfied at a single node, this minimal directory node could determine the node to which the request should be sent. This node type could provide the basis for a centralized directory function. One reason for centralizing this function would be security. If all the requests were forwarded to a central directory node, then the other nodes in the network would not have to know either the identity or the location of the various nodes that make up the network.

A minimal directory node could only determine the logical node identifiers. It could not actually do the routing because it would not have the network description. In this case the request and the logical node identifier would have to be sent to still another node at which the actual routing could be done. Though possible, this is not a very practical division of labor. Therefore, an obvious enhancement for a minimal directory node is to include the network description. This would allow the node also to route the request once it had determined the appropriate logical node identifier. Even this configuration could still only process remote requests. Unless there were another copy of the network data directory at a more complete node, this would probably restrict the entire system to local and remote requests. The decomposition of compound requests requires the network data directory. Therefore, another clear enhancement is to include the necessary additional functions so that the node could also decompose a compound request and determine the network-wide strategy for processing it. These types of enhancements would be providing more of the NDBMS functions at the node. This can be done while still isolating the node from both the users and the database.

Minimal Network Description (Routing) Node

This is the final type of minimal node. It provides only the routing function, which is probably the least likely to be found isolated at a minimal node. The minimal routing function would be to take the physical node identifier, determine a routing, and send the message. The conversion from a logical node identifier to a physical node identifier or address would have to have been done earlier at another node. In practice, this type of node would probably have to accept the logical node identifier, determine the physical node identifier, and do the routing. The next logical step would be to include the functions of the minimal network directory node. Therefore, in practice these last two minimal-node types would probably be combined.

Database Computer Node

The database computer node is a specialized type of node. Today in a centralized environment, database computer (DBC) technology is progressing very rapidly.[2,3] In the future, the DBC node should become relatively common in many networks. In a centralized environment, the DBC concept involves a general purpose host doing the application processing, while the database management functions are off-loaded to a separate DBC. The DBC can be implemented using either general purpose or special purpose hardware, but the most effective approach involves special purpose hardware designed specifically for the database management functions. The DBC, regardless of how it is implemented, is used to off-load some or all of the database management functions from the host. In a centralized environment, the DBC controls the database, its definitions (including the schema and all of the subschemas), and all the DBMS functions. All the operations done on the database are done through the DBC.

Figure 7–2 shows the functions of a centralized local DBMS. The expanding blocks indicate larger sets of functions that can be off-loaded to a DBC. There are two obvious extremes. At one, there is simply the intelligent controller or disk that searches for and retrieves records based on specific key value. At the other, there is the full database computer that accepts high-level queries from a host, does all the processing, and returns the final response. Because of the communications speeds and overhead, all the current DBC work assumes that the DBC interfaces with the host through a high-level query language. This assumption is made even though today most of the DBC work is being done in a centralized environment in which these communications links can be channel to channel and therefore much faster than those in most DDBMSs.

Although most of the DBC work has been in a centralized system, it can easily be extended into the distributed environment and applied to a DDBMS. In doing this, two issues arise, one of which concerns function placement. The other issue involves data placement and the existence of multiple DBCs in a distributed system.

As with a centralized environment, the first issue that must be resolved in a distributed system is to determine which functions to off-load to the DBC. The database management functions that are currently assumed to reside on the DBC are the functions of a centralized DBMS. In a distributed system these functions are performed partly by the local DBMS and partly by the NDBMS. There is no question about off-loading the functions that are being performed by the local DBMS. These are the functions that would be assigned to a DBC even in a centralized system, as follows:

1. Determine the local processing strategy.
2. Locate the data in the logical data structure.
3. Locate the data in the physical data structure.

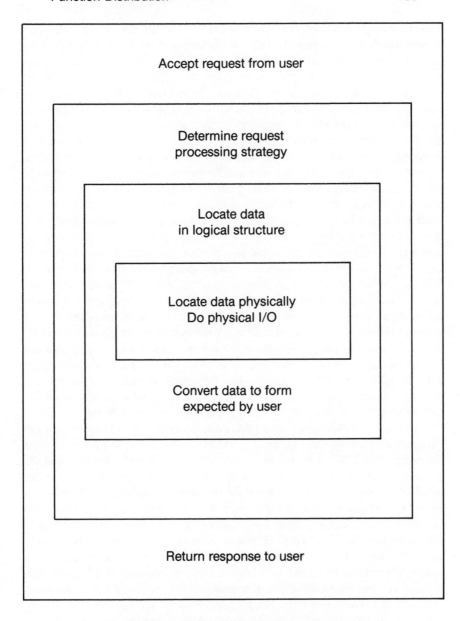

Figure 7–2. Functional Layers of DBMS

4. Do the physical I/O.
5. Convert the data to the form expected by the user.

Therefore, the real issue in the first area is where to place the NDBMS and communications functions and how to connect the DBC to the network. The answer depends on whether the DBC is implemented using special purpose or general purpose hardware. If the DBC is implemented using special purpose hardware, then it was designed to optimize the inherently parallel nature of many of the database management functions. In this case the NDBMS functions and the communications functions should not be placed on the DBC because they would not make effective use of its parallel architecture. This type of DBC should, therefore, be connected to the network through a general purpose processor. The DBC node would be similar to a centralized DBC system with a general purpose host connected to a special purpose backend DBC. The node would be connected to the network through the general purpose host, which would perform all of the NDBMS and communications functions. If, on the other hand, the DBC is implemented on a general purpose architecture, then the use of a general purpose host is not necessary. The DBC could be directly connected to the network and could also perform the NDBMS and communications functions. In this case the decision of which functions to off-load to the DBC would depend more on its processing power than on its architecture; thus the systems designer would have much greater flexibility. Considering probably future developments, such as more special purpose architectures, the system designer should only off-load the local DBMS functions and connect the DBC to the network through a general purpose host. This approach provides the benefit of easily upgrading to a special purpose DBC when it becomes available. If the design assumes that the DBC is a general purpose processor and that other functions are placed on it, then a significant redesign may be necessary to make use of any DBC involving special purpose architecture.

The second issue raised by a DBC node concerns data placement and the existence of multiple DBC nodes. The simplest approach is to place the entire database at one DBC node, but this limits both the size of the database and the processing power of the DBMS. A single copy of the database also reduces the reliability of the system. However, if the database is distributed to many nodes by either partitioning or replication, then the DBC becomes just another node in a distributed database management system. In some cases, however, one of the major benefits of a DBC is that it permits a centralized rather than a distributed solution to a database problem. This could occur either because the increased performance of the DBMS on a DBC or because the DBC provides a single access path to the database so that multiple hosts can access the same database. All the current DBC literature and systems assume this type of centralized situation. The only situation in which they consider multiple DBCs is if the database can be partitioned so that all requests are either local or remote. If compound requests are required either to process jointly data in two or more partitions of the database or to synchronize an update of replicated data, then all the problems involved in distributed database management can occur. If this happens, then the DBC becomes just another node in the system. In this case part of the database may be stored under a DBC, whereas the rest of it is stored at other nodes that consist of only general purpose processors rather than DBCs. In this case the only benefit the DBC provides is improved performance.

Complete Node

A complete node has all the functions described in section 7–1. It has a user interface, at least part of the database, a complete definition for the data it contains, and all the functions of both the NDBMS and the local DBMS. It also has both the network data directory and the network description, if these components exist. However, a complete node must have a significant amount of processing power and storage capacity to provide all of these functions. A DDBMS consisting of only complete nodes provides a simpler conceptual design than a heterogeneous system that may have many different node types. In any system the designer must keep track of where the data are placed, how to decompose the requests, and how to synchronize the updating of multiple copies of the data. In a heterogeneous system, he must also keep track of which functions are needed at specific points in the processing and where those functions are placed.

A complete node has all the functions of a distributed database management system, but only within the context of a specific implementation. For example, if a design does not allow replicated data, then the complete node in that system would not have a complex set of synchronization procedures. However, if the design allowed replication, then the complete node would have those functions, even if that particular node did not contain data that were replicated elsewhere.

7–3. Summary

This chapter has described function placement—a topic frequently ignored in current discussions of distributed database management systems. It began by providing a list of functions that must be performed to process a transaction. These functions are performed by the NDBMS, the local DBMS, and the communications software.

The second section identified several ways in which these functions can be clustered to create certain types of nodes. For each of the node configurations, three areas were covered: (1) what functions were included, (2) what data were required to perform these functions, and (3) other functions and data that could be added to the node to enhance its capability.

In discussing the various functions, update synchronization and query decomposition were mentioned but not described in any detail because of their complexity. The next two chapters discuss these functions in much greater detail.

Notes

1. CODASYL Systems Committee, *A Framework for Distributed Database Systems: Distributed Alternatives and Generic Architectures,* (New York: Association for Computing Machinery, 1981).

2. O.H. Bray and H.A. Freeman, *Data Base Computers* (Lexington, Mass.: Lexington Books, D.C. Heath and Company, 1979).

3. O.H. Bray "Data Base Computers: A New Generation of Backend Storage Subsystems," *Proceedings of the Hawaii International Conference on System Sciences* (January 1981).

8   Update Synchronization

One of the main purposes of database management is to allow multiple users to share data. As long as all the users are only retrieving data, there is no problem. If several of the users are also updating the database, however, a synchronization problem can occur. Updating can create an accuracy problem or a consistency problem. If two users each try to update the same data item at the same time, then one of the updates is lost and the accuracy of the database is impaired. The consistency problem arises when a single update transaction involves updating several data items. In this case, either all the items must be updated, or none of them should be updated. The consistency problem occurs if only some of them are done. In a centralized system, consistency must be maintained among the various parts of the database. In a distributed system this may be only part of the consistency problem. If there are several copies of the database, not only must the internal consistency of each copy be maintained, but consistency must also be maintained among the various copies of the database. Collectively these three problems (maintaining database accuracy with concurrent updates to the same data item, maintaining the internal consistency of the database, and maintaining the consistency among the various copies of the database) are referred to as the update synchronization problem.

This chapter explains the update synchronization problem and describes some of the main methods that have been proposed to resolve it. The first section explains the basic problem and describes how to solve it in a centralized system. This section provides the background for the rest of the chapter because in the distributed environment, the basic problem is still present, although in a complicated form, and most of the proposed solutions involve various extensions of the centralized solution. The second section describes the additional complexity that is created in a distributed system. If an update involves replicated data, the required synchronization procedures are much more complicated. The next four sections discuss different methods for solving the update synchronization problem. Some of these alternatives provide general solutions, whereas others are applicable only if certain constraints are placed on the system. Section 8–3 describes the global-locking procedure, which is the most straightforward extension of the centralized approach. This procedure provides a general solution that can solve the synchronization problem in all situations. Unfortunately, it is very time consuming and expensive and therefore, is not practical except in special cases. The other procedures attempt to improve the cost-performance and response time of updates by reducing the generality of the solution. For example, section 8–4 discusses the dominant copy approach, which limits the way in which updates can be done. With this approach, the response time for an update is partly dependent on the node at which it enters the system. Section 8–5 describes the majority consensus approach, which uses timestamps as an alternative to locking the data. This method also requires a significant amount of processing and communications overhead. All these methods specify a single synchronization procedure at system design time. All updates must then be synchronized using this method. Section 8–6 describes a variable synchronization protocol method. The system design includes several different synchronization procedures and an algorithm for selecting which one to use for a specific update transaction. By selecting the specific synchronization procedure required for each type of update, the overhead on the entire system can be reduced.

8–1. Concurrency Control in a Centralized System

This section provides the background for the other sections of the chapter by describing the update synchronization problem in a centralized system and the way it is solved. (In a centralized system this problem is often referred to as the concurrency problem.)

In a centralized DBMS, the synchronization problem can occur in two situations. In both cases there is at least one user who is updating the database. There is another user who is trying either to update or to retrieve the same data item. If the two users are both trying to update the same item, then synchronization control is required to prevent their destroying the accuracy and validity of the data. If one user is only retrieving the data, whereas the other one is updating them, then the database itself cannot be damaged unless only part of a multiple update transaction is done, but the retrieval response may be inaccurate or even invalid. Both of these cases are discussed here.

The concurrency problem arises because the update operation is usually a two-step procedure. First, the data are retrieved from the database. They are then modified, and the new value is written back to the database. This two-step operation is required whenever the new value is based on data already stored in the database. For example, the new inventory level is equal to the old level minus the number of units taken out of the inventory. In this case the variable being changed is also the one being used to determine the new value; however, this is not always the case.

In general, an update involve two types of variables—base variables and object variables. An object variable is one that is being modified. A base variable is one whose current value is being used to determine the new value for the object variable. Depending on the complexity of the update transaction, several base and object variables may be involved. These variables could also be in several different records. The important point is that it is not sufficient only to lock the object variables or the records in which they occur. All the base variables must also be locked until the update has been completed. During the update, a retrieval request could access the base variables without risking either invalidating the database or getting an invalid response. Some types of retrievals, such as statistical reporting, could even access the object variables without materially affecting their results. Other types of retrievals, such as for a trial balance, would get an invalid result if they access the object variables during the update. If another user tried to update either the base or the object variables while the first update was still in progress, the integrity and validity of the database could be destroyed.

The "window" during which the concurrency problem can occur is between the time the base variables are read and the time the modified object variables are rewritten. If another user begins processing a request during this "window," he is working with out-of-date data. Consider what can happen when two users are trying to update the database. Assume that two salesmen are selling widgets and removing them from the inventory when they are sold. The first salesman retrieves the inventory count (100 widgets) and begins processing to remove 75 widgets for his order. Then a second salesman retrieves the inventory count (still 100 widgets) and begins to process his order for 50. Now the first salesman completes his processing and writes back what he thinks is the new inventory level (25). The second salesman then completes his processing and writes back what *he* thinks is the new inventory level (50). The effect of the first sale is lost, and the inventory data is now inaccurate.

To avoid this problem, the first user must specify that the data are being retrieved as part of an update. The DBMS then knows to lock the data (that is, all the base and object variables) until the new value has been stored. The updating process is now indivisible so that another user cannot begin processing in the middle of an update. This forces all the updates to be done serially rather than concurrently. If the updating is fast enough, however, the second user will not perceive that he has been delayed by the lock. In other words, to the users it will appear as though they were able to share the data and do their updates at the same time. It is important that the DBMS do this locking transparently to the user. The integrity of the database will be destroyed if the locking is not done correctly. Therefore, the DBMS cannot rely on the users to perform this function.

The transaction used in the foregoing example involved only one record being read and updated. However, more complex logical transactions are possible. The base and object variables may be stored in several records. In this case, all the records must be locked when they are read, and none of the locks can be released until the update is completed.

Some logical update transactions involve updating many individual records.

If a customer ordered several items and the proceudre was either to fill the order completely or to hold it, then the sales routine would need to read and lock the inventory record for each item that was ordered. The inventory level for each item would be modified. The locks would be released once all the items had been updated and the new values had been stored. This example is a straightforward extension of the previous one. However, now a new problem can occur: two transactions can deadlock. One transaction wants to update records X and Y, and another transaction wants to update Y and then X. Each transaction can update its first records, but a deadlock occurs when it tries to update the second record. Neither transaction can continue until the other has completed. To solve the concurrency problem, this deadlock problem must also be solved.

There are two basic approaches to solving the deadlock problem. The first approach is to allow the deadlock to occur and then recover from it. Although deadlock is often difficult to detect, in some cases it is relatively simple to resolve once it has been detected. One of the users is rolled back to where he was before he started the transaction. The changes he had made to the database are eliminated and his locks are released. If user A had a higher priority, then user B would be rolled back to the point before he requested record Y, and record Y would be restored to its value before B's update. Then record Y would be locked for user A who could then proceed. Later user B's update transaction would be reprocessed.

Given the difficulty in detecting a deadlock, the alternate approach is to prevent it from occurring. There are several ways of doing this. Commonly used methods include prespecify, presequence, and preempt. The first method is to prespecify all the resources or data that the transaction will need. The DBMS would not lock any of the data unless they could all be locked. In the foregoing example, user A (or user B) would have asked for and gotten both records X and Y, or he would have gotten neither record. Although this approach may be adequate for a file system, in a database environment the user initially may not know all the data that will be needed to satisfy the request. The second method is to presequence the order in which the data can be requested. With this method both users would have had to request the records in the same sequence, either X and then Y or Y and then X. The third method for avoiding deadlock is to allow a user to be preempted. This method is similar to the method described for deadlock recovery, except that the deadlock is not allowed to occur. The second user's request would be analyzed to determine whether it would cause a deadlock. If it would cause a deadlock, then a decision is made based on the priority of the two requests. If the second request had a lower priority than the first one which already had the data locked, then the second request would be preempted and rolled back to the start of the transaction. If the second request had a higher priority than the first one, the first request would be preempted and rolled back. All the changes it had made would be eliminated, and its locks would be released. The second, higher priority request could then obtain the necessary locks and continue processing.

The various techniques described in this section are sufficient for update synchronization in a centralized DBMS. Additional problems arise in a distributed environment, especially when there are multiple copies of the data and concurrent transactions can enter the system from different nodes. These added complexities are discussed in the next section.

8–2. Update Synchronization in a Distributed Environment

All the problems discussed in the previous section also occur with a distributed database management system. If the DDBMS only allows a partitioned database—that is, a single copy of the data—and local or remote requests, then the foregoing procedures are adequate. Complications arise if the DDBMS allows either compound requests or multiple copies of the data.

With compound requests deadlock problems can occur across nodes, even if the database is only partitioned. A compound request is a single logical transaction. Either the entire request must be completed, or none of it should be done. Therefore, it is similar to the previous example, in which users A and B both needed to process records X and Y. A compound request creates the same problem, but with the added complexity that users A and B may have issued their requests at separate nodes, and records Y and X may be stored at different nodes. In a centralized system the deadlock could be resolved because the DBMS could recognize that it had occurred and roll back one of the transactions. In the distributed case, however, neither node would recognize that a deadlock existed. It is only on a network-wide basis that the NDBMS could determine that a deadlock had occurred. It is much more difficult for the NDBMS to determine whether a deadlock has occurred because it requires extensive processing and communications overhead. The alternative is for the NDBMS to detect when a deadlock could occur and prevent it, rather than wait for it to occur and then recover from it. In fact, this is the procedure used by many of the synchronization algorithms described in later sections.

The other complication in a distributed database environment occurs when there are multiple copies of the data. This is the case with either replicated or hybrid data distribution. With multiple copies of the database, update synchronization has two objectives: first, to maintain the consistency and integrity of the data within a single copy of the database, and second, to maintain the consistency among the various copies of the database. Ideally, the same transaction would not get a different response if it entered the system at a different node and used a different copy of the database. In reality, not many of the synchronization methods do allow this to happen. Only the global locking approach, and in certain cases the dominant copy approach, can guarantee this level of consistency. Because it is very expensive to provide this level of consistency, in many cases the system designers are willing to accept a lower level of consistency, known as *convergent consistency*. At any instant in time the various copies of the database may not be identical (that is, consistent). This means that the same retrieval requests, entered at different nodes, could produce different results. With convergent consistency, if the DDBMS stopped accepting new update requests and completed the requests that were already in the system, then all the copies of the database would converge. In other words, when all the updates currently being processed are completed, all the copies of the database would be identical. Until all the updates are completed, the copies would not be identical. A consequence of using convergent consistency is that it is impossible to determine the most current value for any item in the database, unless all the updates are allowed to complete. This is not a problem with the global locking or the dominant copy synchronization approaches because they use the higher level of consistency.

The next four sections describe various synchronization procedures. The assumption is made that the entire database is replicated at each node; however, this is done purely to simplify the discussion and has little real effect on any of the procedures or the points being made. All the algorithms can be easily modified to accept the partitioned or hybrid data distribution alternative.

8–3. Global Locking

There are many ways in which updates can be synchronized in a distributed database system. The global locking approach is a simple extension of the locking approach used in a centralized system. All the copies of the data are locked, the update is made to every copy, and then all the locks are released. This approach provides the strongest degree of consistency and can be used in any situation. Its only difficulty is in its performance. Communications are expensive and time consuming, and this approach in its simplest form requires five messages for each copy of the data:

1. The requesting node issues a lock request.
2. Each data node responds when the data have been locked.
3. The requesting node then issues the actual update request.
4. Each data node makes the update and responds when it has been completed.
5. The requesting node then sends the command to release the locks.

These five messages are the minimum required for every successful update. The average number of messages per update is greater because some updates are not completed successfully the first time they are attempted. For example, if there were ten copies of the data, a request might succeed in locking nine of them. Another request could have gotten the tenth copy and just started the process of locking all the copies. This would create a deadlock that would have to be resolved. Regardless of how the deadlock is resolved, the effect is that in some cases after locking several copies of the data, a request would have to be rolled back and its locks released. The request would then have to go through all five steps when it was retried later.

There are several ways in which all these messages could be communicated. The two basic communications methods are serial and parallel. The requesting node could use a serial communications method to get the request to all the nodes. Assume that there are four nodes (A, B, C, and D) with the request originating at node A. Using the serial approach, node A would send the request to node B. If the data were already locked at node B, it would return a reject. If node B could lock the data, it would do so and pass the request to node C. Node C would then lock the data and pass the request to node D. Finally, node D would lock the data and return the acknowledgment to node A that all the copies of the data were locked. Similarly, the actual update request and the unlock request could also be transmitted using this serial approach.

The parallel alternative would involve broadcasting the request to all the data nodes. From the DBMS's perspective, the broadcast can be done either logically or physically. With certain communications technologies, it is possible to broadcast a message physically—that is, the requesting node transmits the message once, and all the destination nodes receive this transmission. On the other hand, with other communications technologies the node may only be able to logically broadcast the message to the other nodes. In this case the DBMS instructs the communications software to broadcast the message—that is, send it to all the nodes or to a selected subset of them. If the communications software cannot physically broadcast the message, then it will send individual copies of the message to each node. In either case, as far as the DBMS is concerned, the message has been broadcasted because the DBMS has not had to send a series of individual messages to each node. The requesting node would broadcast each of its three requests (1, 3, and 5). The responding or data node would not need to use the broadcast approach because its messages normally would only need to be sent to the requesting node. By increasing the parallelism with which the locking and updating is done, this broadcast approach would minimize the response time, but at the expense of increasing the number of messages and, therefore, the overhead in the system.

Regardless of whether the serial or parallel communications approach is used, the update synchronization procedure must be reliable. Therefore, the effects of a failure in each step in processing the request must be considered. Either a node or a communications link can fail; however, only a node failure is described here. This limitation is reasonable because if the only link to a node or all the links to a node fail, then the effect is the same as that of a failure of the node: the node will not receive and process the request. If only one of several links to a node fails, then the communications system should automatically reroute the message so the node would receive it over one of the remaining links. A failure could involve either the requesting node or one of the data nodes. Both cases are considered in this section. If a node does not respond to a request, either because the node itself failed or because there was a failure of one or more communications links that isolated the node from the network, then its copy of the data becomes out of date, and certain recovery procedures are required.

There are two ways for the system to recognize a failure. First, a node can recognize that a failure has occurred and explicitly notify the system. Once the node has been repaired, it is reconnected to the system and goes through the necessary recovery prcedures. The other way for a failure to be recognized is through a time-out. If a node fails to respond within a given period of time, it is assumed to have failed. The difficulty with this method is that the system cannot unambiguously distinguish between a real failure and simply an unexpectedly long delay in responding. Once the recovery procedures are begun, they must be completed, even if subsequently the expected response is received.

When a failure is recognized, two types of recovery actions are necessary. The system must immediately take recovery action so that it can continue to operate despite the failure. This action involves rolling back and restarting any affected transactions. It also involves flagging the node (or communications link) as failed so that the system does not continue to try to use it and get more failure responses. The system may periodically test the node to see whether it has been repaired and is now available, or the node may send a message to the system when it has been repaired and is ready to begin its local recovery. In addition to the immediate recovery procedures that the network must perform in order to continue operating, there are also certain recovery procedures that the node must perform once it has been repaired. These include rolling back any partial transactions that were left hanging, making any adjustments for actions taken during the network recovery, and bringing its out-of-date copy of the database forward to the current state. Only after all of this local recovery has been done is the node fully recovered and ready to resume its normal operation within the network.

The rest of this section discusses the reliability of the global locking synchronization method for the parallel and serial communications approaches. In either case, any failure of the requesting node before the initial lock request is issued requires only local recovery once the node has been repaired. Since no request would have yet been issued, the failure would have no network-wide effects. The following paragraphs consider the reliability of the parallel communications approach. Subsequent paragraphs then discuss the reliability of the serial approach.

In the parallel case, the requesting node could fail between the time its communications software sent the lock request to the first node and the time the lock request was sent to the last node. (Obviously, this could only happen if the system were using logical rather than physical broadcasting.) The effect is that some of the copies of the data would be locked but that some of them would not be locked. The nodes that locked their copies of the data would have sent an acknowledgment, but the subsequent update and unlock commands would not have been issued because of the failure of the requesting node. At this point, there are two alternate actions that one of the nodes that had received a lock request could take. In both these cases, a time-out is used at the locked node. If a certain period of time passes after the node returns the lock acknowledgment and the requesting node does not follow up with the actual update request, then the locked node can assume that the requesting node has failed. The simplest approach is for one of the locked nodes to broadcast a command to abort the request and notify the requesting node. When the requesting node has been repaired and recovered, it would have to reissue the request. The system would be more reliable, however, if the locked node that recognized the failure of the requesting node took over the control of the request and completed it. This approach is possible only if the initial lock request includes the entire request. This backup copy of the request could be sent to only a few or to all the nodes that contain copies of the data.

The other problem that could occur at the beginning of an update transaction is that one of the data nodes could fail before it processed the lock request and sent the acknowledgment back to the requesting node. In this case the requesting node would get too few lock acknowledgments. A time-out could be used to indicate that one of the nodes had failed. It is important that the failure of the data node not prevent the request from being processed at the other nodes. If it did, then the failure of any node would prevent all updates. Therefore, the request should be processed at the other nodes even though one node has failed and has to be recovered later. For this to be possible, each data node must respond to a lock request. The response may be either an accept or a reject (if the data are already locked); but there must always be a response for the time-out to be used.

Similar problems can occur if the requesting node fails while it is issuing the actual update request, or a data node fails before it can acknowledge the update. In both these cases the solutions are comparable to those just described. Using a time-out, a data node can recognize the failure of the requesting node and either abort the request or take over control and complete it. The requesting node would use a time-out to recognize the failure of a data node that did not acknowledge the update. The request would still be completed and the failed data node would complete processing the update during its recovery procedure.

Finally, either the requesting or the data node could fail while the unlock request was being issued. A long period following the update request without an unlock request would indicate to a data node the probable failure of the requesting node. At this point the data node could check with the other data nodes and, if any of them had received an unlock request, then all the nodes could go ahead and unlock the data and the update would be complete. To ensure that the update transaction has been completed, at least one data node must have received the unlock request. Without this unlock command or commitment from the requesting node, there is no guarantee that the one or more updates a node has already received are not simply part of a longer uncompleted logical update transaction. If none of the nodes had yet received an unlock request, then either the update would have to be backed out and the data unlocked, or another node would have to take control of the request and complete it. The recovery of the requesting node would differ depending on which procedure was used; but the choice of procedure would be made at system design time and an appropriate recovery procedure would be included in the system. Notice that if any failures do occur, then far more than the usual five messages per copy are required for the update.

The following paragraphs consider the reliability of the serial communications approach. The pure serial approach (where node A sends a message to node B, node B sends it to node C, node C to node D, and so forth) is very unreliable. If any node fails before it sends the message on, then the message is lost or at least delayed until the node has been repaired and recovered. Therefore, what is called a serial approach in this section is really a hybrid. Each node sends every message to at least two nodes. In general, a node could send each message to N nodes, with the reliability of the system increasing as N gets larger. In the extreme case, where N equals the number of nodes, the hybrid approach becomes the parallel approach. The way in which this type of communications improves the system reliability is shown in the discussion of the lock request.

The requesting node sends the lock request to two nodes. Each subsequent node also sends the message to two nodes. If the requesting node sends the lock request to nodes A and B, they would each lock the data and send both the lock request and their acknowlgedment to two additional nodes. Although each node should get two copies of the lock request, it can actually lock its data and pass the request on to the next two nodes as soon as it gets the first request. By not waiting for the second copy of the request, the node can reduce the overall response time for the system. When the second copy is received, the node does not have to do anything. If the second copy is not received within a certain time-out period after the first one, the assumption is that the node that was to send the second copy has failed. Therefore, when a single node has failed, the system not only can continue to operate but also can determine which node has failed. This allows the update to continue to be processed. In general, if each node sends N copies of the message, then the system can lose $(N-1)$ nodes and can continue to operate and still isolate the failed nodes. If a node cannot lock the data (because another request has already locked them), then it sends a reject rather than an acknowledgment. For performance reasons, the reject would probably be broadcast rather than transmitted serially. The requesting node must then release its locks and try again after a certain time delay. If the wait before retrying is different for each node in the system, then the probability is very low that the same two requests would also conflict the next time they were tried. From this discussion it should be apparent how this approach could process a failure at any point in the update transaction.

Other than for reliability, which is higher for the parallel approach, the trade-off between the serial and parallel approaches is that the serial approach requires fewer messages and, therefore, less overhead, but at the expense of increasing the response time for the update transaction.

Because of the characteristics of global locking, this approach allows any node to accept and control an update request for any of the data. In the hybrid data distribution case, this still applies even if the requesting node does not have a copy of the data.

Although global locking does provide adequate synchronization, it has a very high overhead. The following three sections discuss alternate synchronization methods that attempt to reduce this overhead in certain special cases.

8-4. Dominant Copy Synchronization

The dominant copy synchronization method provides a relatively simple, low-overhead means of synchronizing updates when there are multiple copies of the data.[1,2] It could be used with either a replicated or a hybrid database distribution alternative. However, it is appropriate only for certain patterns of data usage. Ideally, there should be a fairly high locality of reference for the updates and a relatively low frequency of updates. Finally, the updates should not be particularly time critical since they may require a significantly greater response time than the retrievals. The reasons for these constraints become apparent as the method is explained. As in the previous section, assume that the database is completely replicated. Although this is not necessary, it does simplify the discussion.

The key characteristic of the dominant copy approach that distinguishes it from all the other synchronization methods is that all the copies of the data are not equal. One copy of the data is defined as the *dominant copy*. (The node at which this copy is stored is called the *dominant node*.) Any update of the data must be sent to this node, which controls all the updates for any of the data for which it is the dominant node. Eventually, all the copies of the data would be updated, but the dominant copy is always the first one to be updated, regardless of where the update request originated. Retrievals, on the other hand, could be performed at any node that has a copy of the data. If there were a very large volume of update transactions, the dominant node could become a bottleneck. This is why the dominant copy approach is applicable only if there are relatively few updates or if the updates are not time critical.

The dominant copy for different parts of the database can be stored at different nodes. This means that once the NDBMS has determined what data is to be updated, it must then determine where the dominant copy for that data is stored. This would not be particularly difficult because it requires only an additional flag in the network data directory. The only limitation is that any update request must be completely satisfied at the node with the dominant copy. For example, assume a fully replicated database with the dominant copy for part A at node 1 and the dominant copy of part B at node 2. All update requests must use only data in part A or only data in part B. No update request could involve some data in part A and some data in part B. All the base and object variables must be in the same part. Therefore, the way in which dominant copies are allocated to the various nodes affects the type of update transactions that are acceptable. This limitation exists because of the way locking is done with the dominant copy approach.

With the global locking approach, every copy of the data had to be locked before the update could be made. Although this required extensive communications overhead, it was necessary because an update transaction could begin at any node. With the dominant copy approach, much of this communications is eliminated because only the dominant copy is locked. All the update requests must begin processing and be controlled by the node with the dominant copy of the data. An update request could still enter the system at any node, but if it entered at a node that did not have the dominant copy, it would not be processed there but would be routed to the node with the dominant copy. The actual update processing would begin at that point. Thus, as long as the dominant copy of the data is locked, any updates to that data are forced to be serialized. A second update cannot begin on the same data until the previous update is completed. This ensures that while it is being done, any update is indivisible, thereby ensuring the integrity and consistency of the database.

Once the dominant node has updated the dominant copy of the data, it then controls the updating of all of the other copies of the data. The response time for the update transaction is also improved because once the dominant copy has been modified (and the change has been logged), the node requesting the update can be notified that it has been completed. In practice, however, the local copy of the data should also be modified before the user is informed that the request is completed. This would allow the user to retrieve the data and get the new value immediately. Otherwise, it would be possible for the user to request and obtain the data before his local copy was updated. This could result in the user being told that the update was completed, but then being given a copy of the data that did not reflect the update. The simplest approach, but the one with the greatest response time, is not to notify the user that the update has been made until all of the copies are updated. This would solve the problem for one node. In general, however, data that are retrieved from a nondominant copy may be out of date. Even before a user retrieves a local copy of the data, the dominant copy of that data may have already been updated. However, the dominant copy approach provides an advantage over the global locking approach. By requesting that the retrieval be done from the dominant copy, a user can be assured of getting the latest version of the data. If the request is made at the dominant node, this occurs automatically. A user at any node can still obtain this latest version, however, as long as he specifies that the retrieval should be done against the dominant copy and is willing to pay the price (that is, increased response time).

From the description so far, there appears to be one serious problem with the reliability of the dominant copy approach. What happens if the node with the dominant copy fails? For reliability, there must be a way to allow another copy to become the dominant copy if anything happens to the dominant node.

To be able to recover if the dominant node fails, certain precautions must have been taken ahead of time. First, a backup node must have been designated. Depending on the degree of fault tolerance that is required, any number of backup nodes can be designated. As more backup nodes are assigned, the reliability of the system increases—but so does its overhead. In the extreme case, if every node is a backup, then the dominant copy approach is even less efficient than the other methods. In principle, if a node has the dominant copy for several parts of the database, the backup node for each part could be different; but this generally could greatly complicate the recovery procedure. Whenever an update request enters the system, it is sent to the appropriate dominant node. Before the dominant copy is actually updated, the node sends a backup copy of the request to its backup node. If everything is processed normally, then this backup copy of the request is ignored. However, the backup node uses a time-out to determine whether the dominant node is in operation and is processing the request. If the backup node does not receive the processed request from the dominant node within a certain period, it assumes that the dominant node has failed and notifies all the nodes that it is now the dominant node for the appropriate part of the database. It would then transmit a backup copy of all of the pending requests that had not been processed by the failed dominant node and would begin processing them. If at a later point the backup node failed, then *its* backup node could take over. With this approach any number of dominant nodes could fail, and the update requests still could be processed as long as a copy of the data was still available.

Now that a procedure has been described for shifting the dominant-copy status when the dominant node fails, the other failure points and their effects must be considered. If the node at which the update transaction originated failed before it issued the request, then there is no impact on the network and the node would simply issue the request once it was repaired and recovered. If the requesting node failed after the request was issued and accepted by the dominant node, then the request could still be completed and the node would be given the status information once it was back on line. This is because the dominant node takes over control of the update request so that the subsequent failure of the requesting node does not affect the completion of the update. If the requesting node were the dominant node, then the backup node would take over and complete the request. In some cases a logical update transaction (identified by an explicit begin and end) involves several separate requests, and the requesting node could fail between these separate requests. The dominant node would use a time-out to determine whether the requesting node had failed. If it had, the dominant node would then have to abort the request because it would not have received all the requests that make up the complete transaction. However, once the dominant node has received the complete update transaction, the failure of any node in the system does not affect the completion of the request. The dominant node (or its replacement, if it fails) will ensure that every node with a copy of the data receives the complete update transaction and acknowledges that it has been completed. The failure of any node with a copy of the data is also irrelevant. If the node fails after it has updated its local copy of the data, there is no problem. If it fails before it is able to update its local copy, then the update will be made as part of the node's local recovery procedure. However, it is important for the dominant node to realize that a data node has failed and reduce the number of responses it expects. If this change is not made as part of the immediate network-level recovery, then as long as the component remains down, the system would wait for the time-out to expire on each transaction and then do a recovery.

In summary, the dominant copy approach to update synchronization provides significant performance improvements over the global locking method. To accomplish this, certain simplifying assumptions are necessary. These assumptions concern the pattern of use of the data. This approach is normally acceptable only if certain conditions are met. The first condition is that there is a relatively low update frequency. The second condition is that the database can be partitioned so that most updates have a high locality of reference—that is, most of the updates for a particular part of the data are from a specific node. Finally, most of the nodes that require only retrievals for data for which they are not the dominant node should not need the dominant copy of the data (that is, the most current version of the data). For example, consider a company with a computerized inventory system. Each warehouse would have the dominant copy of its own inventory, but other warehouses and some of the sales offices could also have copies of its data. If a user wants to know the inventory level—for example, if a salesman wants to know if an order can be filled—he can query the local copy of the data. In most cases it is irrelevant whether the inventory is actually 200 or 195, as long as the answer is current enough that a tentative decision can be based on it. For the dominant copy approach to work, there must be an acceptable trade-off between the requirement for timely information and the cost of obtaining it.

There are cases in which the constraints imposed by the dominant copy approach are unacceptable. The next two sections discuss approaches that could be used in these situations—for example, where there is no locality of reference. These approaches provide different trade-offs between performance, the timeliness of the data, and the constraints on the system.

8–5. Majority Consensus Synchronization

The global locking procedure requires that all the nodes with copies of the data approve an update before it can be accepted. This approval is given by having each node lock the data involved in the update. The majority consensus approach uses timestamps instead of locks.[3] All the nodes still can vote whether or not to accept the request, but as soon as a majority of the nodes vote to accept it (assuming that no node has rejected it up to that time), then the update can be done. Compared with the global locking approach, the majority consensus approach reduces both the response time for the update and the amount of communications required to coordinate it. Although the dominant copy approach would have a better performance than the majority consensus method, the key performance comparison should be with the global locking approach, which provides a more comparable set of capabilities. Both the global locking and the majority consensus approaches allow update requests to be processed from any node in the system. Neither distinguishes among the various copies of the data, as is done with the dominant copy approach.

The cost that must be paid for these performance improvements is the added storage required for the timestamps. As the method was proposed by Thomas, every field in the database had a timestamp. This would require a tremendous amount of additional storage for a very large database. To reduce the amount of extra storage and some of the processing overhead, the timestamps could be applied at the record level instead. The effect would be similar to locking at the record level rather than at the item level. Some needless conflicts would be incurred and some updates would be delayed, but the probability of such occurrences would be relatively small. Also these occurrences would only result in delaying the update but would not damage the database or affect its integrity.

Thomas defines six steps in an update transaction, as follows:

1. Retrieve the base variables.
2. Compute the new value for the object variables.
3. Submit the update request.
4. Execute the synchronization protocol.
5. Make the update.
6. Notify the originating node and the user of the results.

The first step is to query the database and retrieve the base variables to be used to determine the new value for the update. (The equivalent in most current centralized DBMSs is to retrieve with a lock for a subsequent update.) If the database is replicated, which Thomas assumes, this is always a local request. If the database is not replicated, then it is possible that the base variables are not stored locally. In this case the retrieval request would be a remote or compound request, but the processing would be essentially the same. In either case, the base variables and their timestamps are retrieved. The timestamps indicate to the system when the variables were last modified. These timestamps must be maintained by the system, not the user, because incorrect modification or use of the timestamps could destroy the integrity of the database. The update request must specify the base and object variables so that the system will know which timestamps are needed to synchronize the update properly.

The second step in processing the update is to do the necessary calculations to determine the new values of the object variables. The third step is for the application to issue the actual update request. Fourth, the NDBMS and the various local DBMSs must coordinate their activity to synchronize the update. This is the key step in the majority consensus approach and requires both a voting procedure and a request resolution rule, both of which are described in more detail later. The fifth step, performing the update, occurs only if the request is accepted. The final step is to notify the user of the results of the update request—that is, that it has been accepted and completed or that it has been rejected for some reason.

When a node receives an update request, it usually votes on the request. A node can vote to accept or reject the update or to pass. Under certain conditions discussed later, the node may defer voting. It decides how to vote by examining the timestamps for the base variables. It compares the timestamps on its local copy of the base variables with the corresponding timestamps that were provided in the update request. If any one of its local timestamps is greater (that is, more recent) than the corresponding timestamp in the request, then the requested update is based on obsolete data and must be rejected. In this case the node broadcasts a reject, the request is aborted, and the user is notified. When a reject occurs, the entire request must be reprocessed. It is not sufficient simply to reissue the request. Unless step 1 is repeated, a new timestamp is not attached to the base variables, and the request would be rejected again.

A node would vote to accept a request if its local timestamps on all the base variables were earlier than those in the request and if none of the base variables were object variables for any pending requests. A pending request is one that the node has already voted to accept but has not yet performed because a majority of the nodes have not yet accepted it. These two conditions ensure that the node will not accept a request whose base variables are out of date or may be rendered out of date by a pending request. If the request conflicts with a pending request, the node takes one of two actions depending on the relative priorities of the two requests. (Every request is assigned a priority when it is issued.) If the pending request has a higher priority than the current one, then the node votes to pass. This notifies the other nodes of a potential deadlock between two requests. If the priority of the current request is greater than or equal to the pending request, then the node does not vote.

Once a node has decided how to vote, it must go through a request resolution procedure to determine what action to take. It can decide simply to transmit the request on to another node. This is the only action that it would take, except in three cases. The first of these is a reject vote. If the node votes to reject the update request because it has some base variables with a later timestamp than those in the request, then it broadcasts the reject to all the nodes in the system. The second special case occurs when a node votes to pass and then determines that it is no longer possible for the request to obtain a majority of accept votes and eventually to be accepted. When a node passes a request on to another node, it includes the cumulative results of the voting. This allows any node to decide when it is no longer possible for the request to obtain a majority acceptance. The node then broadcasts a reject to all the nodes and informs the user. The third special case occurs when the node's vote to accept the request is the one that creates the majority. In this case the node broadcasts a message to all the other nodes that the request has been accepted so that they can perform the update.

Once a definite decision has been made either to accept or to reject the request, all the nodes are notified. If the request has been rejected, then each node deletes it from the queue and reevaluates any requests that conflicted with it—that is, those requests for which it either voted pass or did not vote. If any of these requests now becomes acceptable, a node can change its vote on them. If this new vote to accept creates a majority for another request, then the reevaluating node notifies the rest of the nodes that a majority has been reached and the request is accepted. When a node is notified that a request has been accepted, it takes two actions. First, it rejects any pending requests that conflict with the accepted request and notifies all the other nodes. Second, it then applies the accepted update request according to a specific update application rule.

The update application rule determines the action a node needs to take to implement an update. The node must compare the timestamps on its copy of the object variables with the corresponding timestamps in the request. If the local timestamp is earlier, then the update is applied and the new value is stored. The timestamp on the local copy may, however, be later than the timestamp in the request. In this case the update is obsolete and is not performed.

Timestamps are used instead of locks in the majority consensus approach. They serve two critical functions. First, timestamps on the base variables are used by each node to decide whether or not to accept a request. Second, once the update has been accepted, the timestamps on the object variables determine whether or not the update must actually be applied or can be ignored.

A problem can arise in generating the timestamps since the algorithm fails if two or more timestamps can be equal. In a centralized system the internal clock provides the single source of the timestamps. In a distributed system each node has its own clock, and it is very difficult to synchronize them precisely to ensure that there is a single network-wide clock. To solve this problem, Thomas proposes a timestamp consisting of a combination of time and node identification. Once a node has generated a timestamp, it cannot generate another one until its internal clock has been incremented. Different nodes could generate timestamps with the same time value, but then the node identification would be different, so the complete timestamps still would not be equal. These two conditions ensure that two timestamps will never be equal. The node at which a request originates assigns a timestamp to it. To provide some coordination among nodes, each node always checks its internal clock against the time part of the timestamp for every request it receives. If the request has a later timestamp than the local internal clock, then the local clock is reset to the later value.

The rest of this section discusses the reliability of the majority consensus approach. The first criterion is that if a node with a copy of the data fails or becomes isolated and is not available to synchronize an update, the system must still be able to operate with the remaining nodes. This presents no problem. The algorithm assures that a request can be accepted as long as a majority of the nodes vote to accept it.

The second reliablity issue concerns the communications system. The way the majority consensus procedure has been described previously, the communications is assumed to use a daisy-chain procedure. As with the global locking approach, this increases the response time for the transaction but reduces the load on the communications system. The difference is that in this case the request can be sent only to one other node at a time. Because each node must know the voting results from the previous nodes in order to determine what to do after it votes, a node cannot send the request to two or more other nodes to improve the reliability of the system in the event of a node failure. The basic procedure is for each node to use a time-out to determine whether the node to which it sent the request has failed. If there is no response, then the sending node could retry transmitting the request several times. Ultimately, if the destination node has really failed, then the request must be sent to an alternate destination node, and the attempt to obtain a majority will continue. If the majority is obtained, then the update will be made and flagged to be done by the failed node once it has been repaired and returned on line.

In most communications situations, the receiving node acknowledges a message as soon as it is received. Then it processes the request and sends any necessary further response. In this case, however, the receiving node does not acknowledge the request until it has already been processed and sent on to the next node. The original requesting node (and each subsequent node that passes the message on) would know something was wrong if it did not obtain an acknowledgment for its request. At this point it could send the request to another node to continue the processing. Therefore, a reliable communications procedure could be implemented using a modified daisy-chain procedure.

The majority-consensus approach could also be implemented using a broadcast communications procedure, which, however, must be modified. With the broadcast approach, each node does not know how the previous nodes have voted. The node at which the request originated would broadcast the request to all the other nodes. Each node would do the same type of analysis, decide how to vote and return its vote to the requesting node. The requesting node would then do the request resolution procedure to determine whether to accept or reject the request. As soon as it received a vote to reject or the last vote needed to create a majority for acceptance, the requesting node could then transmit the command to accept or reject the request. If the request were accepted, then each node would use the update application rule to determine how to process the update. As with the daisy-chain approach, the failure of any node does not affect the algorithm. However, to survive the failure of the requesting node, the request must also be sent to one or more backup nodes. Any node that received a copy of the request (all the nodes in a replicated system) could function as a backup node; thus reliability, in this case, simply requires a procedure for one of the other nodes to realize that the requesting node has failed. This could be done with a simple time-out between any two messages from the requesting node—for example, the request for a vote and the announcement of the results of the vote. Therefore, the broadcast approach could also be implemented in a fault-tolerant way.

Thomas claims the algorithm is adequate for several reasons. First, the copies of the database converge to the same value. Second, any request is either accepted or rejected. In no case will a request be accepted and processed by some nodes and rejected by others. Third, for accepted updates the algorithm results in mutual exclusion, although locking is not explicitly used. Fourth, since a node is able to vote to pass or to defer voting, the algorithm cannot deadlock. Finally, the way in which the timestamps are constructed and used prevents any sequencing problems.

This approach and the two previous ones have specified a procedure for synchronizing updates and forced all the updates to be synchronized using this method. The next approach provides greater flexibility. It provides several different synchronization procedures, each with a different amount of processing and communications overhead. It also specifies a decision rule for selecting which procedure should be used for which type of update transaction.

8–6. Multiple Protocol Synchronization

This synchronization approach differs from the previous ones in that it uses different protocols for different types of transactions. It is the approach taken by the system for distributed databases–1 (SDD-1), an experimental system being developed by the Computer Corporation of America (CCA). This section summarizes the CCA approach for a completely replicated case.[4,5] The bibliography provides a list of references that addresses specific aspects of SDD-1 in much greater detail.

The basic assumption underlying this approach is that different types of transactions require different levels of synchronization. Since more complex levels of synchronization require greater processing and communications overhead, the overall performance of the system can be improved by identifying those transactions that can use simpler procedures. These transactions can then be done with much less overhead. A key to this approach is a careful analysis of the various transaction types, which must be done when the database is designed. This is an additional function that the database administrator (DBA) must perform. This analysis is used to build a transaction-class table that the NDBMS uses to determine which synchronization protocol to use for each type of transaction. The transaction-class table is built when the database is designed, but it is used when requests are being executed.

Transactions are classified according to their read and write sets—that is, the data they retrieve and update. (Read and write sets in this approach are similar to base and object variables in the majority consensus approach.) These sets are defined by simple boolean selection expressions. One of these sets may include all of the records of a particular type, a subset of records of a particular type, or only certain fields within a set of records. Although read and write sets can be defined arbitrarily, these decisions should be made very carefully. In defining read and write sets, there is a trade-off very similar to the one that must be made in determining the granularity of locks to be used in a locking protocol. If the sets are smaller, there will be more of them and it will take longer to classify each transaction, but there will be fewer conflicts. On the other hand, a few, large sets would reduce some of the processing, but there would be more conflicts that would force the transactions to use a more complex, slower synchronization protocol. This is the reason transaction classification and set definition are so important. A formal analysis should be done to determine which transaction types can conflict and to find the level of synchronization that is needed to prevent conflict for any level of set definition. Any distributed database management system that uses this approach must provide the database administrator with a set of design tools to assist in this design process.

All transactions are processed in two basic steps. First, the transaction is executed locally at the node at which it originated. Second, once the originating node has completed processing the transaction, it issues the commands to the other nodes to process the request. The first step, processing the request at the originating node, may require some synchronization with the other nodes; but they will not begin processing the transaction until the originating node has completed its processing. Before sending any of the synchronization messages needed in step 1, the originating node locks its copy of any of the data it needs. Once the originating node has completed processing the request, it broadcasts the update transaction and its timestamp to all the other nodes. As soon as it has done this, it can release its locks and notify the user that the update request has been completed.

Because timestamps are crucial to all of the SDD-1 synchronization protocols, they are discussed before each of the four protocols is described. Timestamps can be associated with data in the database or with transactions. SDD-1 assumes that every data item in the database has a timestamp. Timestamps are also associated with transactions. Whenever a data item is changed, its timestamp is replaced by the timestamp of the transaction causing the change. The originating node timestamps each transaction when it is entered.

Because timestamps are used to determine a unique sequence in which to perform the updates, no two timestamps can have the same value. Sometimes this is interpreted as requiring a global clock. However, the requirement is not really this rigorous. Instead, uniqueness can be guaranteed by the same two-step procedure that was used by the majority consensus approach for assigning timestamps to transactions. The timestamp is a concatenation of a node's clock time and a node identification number. This combination provides a network-wide unique timestamp for each transaction. All the nodes use this same procedure for generating timestamps. Once an update transaction is accepted, all the nodes also use the timestamps in the same way regardless of which update synchronization protocol is being used. The update application rule is the same as the one used in the majority consensus approach. Each node compares the timestamp on its local copy of the data item to be updated with the timestamp of the update request. If its local timestamp is earlier than the one assigned to the update request, then the new data value replaces the old value. However, if its local timestamp is later than the one attached to the request, then the change is not made. In the latter case the local copy of the data is more recent than the one specified in the update request.

The remainder of this section describes the four synchronization protocols among which the DDBMS can select. These four protocols, P1 through P4, become progressively more complex. Furthermore, each of the protocols uses the simpler ones. For example, the P2 and P3 protocols do some additional processing and then use the P1 procedure. P4 does still more additional processing and then uses the P3 procedure, which in turn uses the P1 procedure.

The first protocol (P1) is used in either of two cases. First, it is used for requests that involve data of local interest. An example would be a warehouse controlling its own inventory. The second case occurs when an update specifies a new value that is independent of any current value—for example, entering a customer's new address. It cannot be used when the new value is in some way dependent on any current value, as in subtract 25 units from the inventory.

This protocol involves four steps. First, the originating node locks its copy of the data involved in the request (that is, the transaction's read and write sets). Second, the update is then made to the local copy. Third, the results of the update are broadcast to all the other nodes in the network. Fourth, the locks are released, and the user is notified that the transaction has been completed. This protocol is very fast for two reasons. Only local locks are needed, and the user is notified that the transaction is completed as soon as the update results are broadcast to the other nodes. This protocol does not wait for an acknowledgment from the other nodes that the request has been processed. Thus, there is a much faster response time. The trade-off is that there is a longer period of time during which a user at another node would get out-of-date data. This trade-off is acceptable either because the data are of primary interest only to the local node or because it is a value-independent update. Usually data items that are modified by value-independent updates are not very volatile. Therefore, the chance of a user at another node obtaining out-of-date data is very small.

Protocols P2 and P3 are very similar. The only difference is in how they determine the timestamp to apply to the transaction. P2 is for retrieval requests for which protocol P1 is not sufficient—for example, one warehouse (A) checking the inventory level at another warehouse (B). In a fully replicated system, this type of request would be relatively rare, since warehouse A could check its own copy of warehouse B's inventory. P3 is for update requests where P1 is not sufficient. P3 could be used for all transactions, but it requires more overhead than either P1 or P2. Therefore, P3 should be used only when the other protocols are not sufficient. System performance is improved if most of the transactions can be done with either P1 or P2.

The difference between P2 and P3 is that the former is used for retrievals and the latter for updates. The only effect this has on the procedure is that the timestamps are selected differently. P2 selects the most recent timestamp in the transaction's read set and assigns it to the transaction. The timestamp of a P3 transaction is set to the current clock time. Beyond this point, both protocols are the same. The next paragraph describes what happens at the node at which the request originated. The three paragraphs that follow describe the actions of the other data nodes.

The originating node accepts the request and sets its timestamp. It then broadcasts a P2/P3 request, which includes the timestamp, to all the other nodes. The originating node waits for a response from all the other nodes before continuing its local processing of the transaction. When each of the other nodes has responded that the request can be accepted, the originating node can process the pending request. The originating node now processes the request using protocol P1—lock the local copy of the data, execute the request, broadcast the request to the other nodes, unlock the local data, and send an acknowledgment to the user. A key point is that with a P2/P3 protocol, a node never rejects a transaction. The most severe action it can take is to delay the transaction until it can be performed correctly. While the originating node is waiting for all the other nodes to accept the P2/P3 request, it can continue processing other requests. The only restriction is that they must have earlier timestamps and not modify the pending transaction's read set. It is irrelevant whether these requests originated locally or were received from other nodes.

Now consider what happens at a node that receives a P2/P3 request. When a node receives a P2/P3 request, any one of three conditions could exist. First, the node may be idle. If it is, then it returns an accept with a timestamp. The timestamp it assigns to the accept is determined by comparing the local clock and the timestamp of the request. The timestamp of the accept is the more recent of the two values. If the timestamp received with the request is later than the current value of the local clock, then the node also resets the local clock to this value.

The other two conditions arise if the receiving node already has a set of requests to process. It will process them in timestamp order. To decide when to acknowledge a new request, the node compares the timestamp of the request it is currently processing with the timestamp of the new request. If the timestamp of the request currently being processed is earlier than the timestamp of the new request, the node finishes the current request. If its queue still has additional requests with earlier timestamps than the new request, these must also be processed before the new request can be accepted. When the new request has the earliest timestamp in the queue, then the receiving node will acknowledge and accept it. Recall that at this point the receiving node is simply accepting the P2/P3 request so that the originating node can begin to process it. At this time the node that has received the P2/P3 request is not going to begin processing it. In fact, it will not begin processing the request until it receives another message from the originating node. When the receiving node acknowledges the P2/P3 request, the timestamp is assigned as described earlier by comparing the local clock and the timestamp assigned to the request.

Finally, if the receiving node is processing a request with a later timestamp than the P2/P3 request, the node can immediately send an accept with a timestamp equal to the one assigned to the request it is currently processing.

Two points should be made about the way a P2/P3 request is processed. First, the update transaction itself is not processed at this point. The P2/P3 request is simply accepted. Once all the other nodes have accepted it, the originating node can complete the processing of the transaction. The second point is that with these two protocols, there is no condition under which the node rejects a request. The most it can do is delay accepting the request. Since a node can only delay and not reject a request, the algorithm is fault tolerant. Assume that a node has failed and cannot accept a P2/P3 request. The update does not have to wait until the node is repaired and restored. First, all the requests that originated at the node before it failed must be processed. Then any new unaccepted requests can be processed, even though they have not been accepted by the failed node. At this point it is safe to process them (assuming they have been accepted by all of the other nodes) because they will now have an earlier timestamp than any subsequent requests from the failed node. Therefore, although the use of timestamps increases the overhead, it does allow the system to be fault tolerant.

The last of the four protocols (P4) is used for unanticipated types of requests. Recall that the transaction-class table was used when the system was designed to classify request types and determine the type of protocol they had to use. Unanticipated requests are those types of transactions that do not fit into one of the predefined classes. Protocol P3 could have been used for all requests, including the unanticipated ones. A more complex P4 protocol is necessary because some transactions are using one of the simpler protocols. P4 is necessary to ensure that the unanticipated transaction will not create problems for those requests currently being processed using one of the simpler protocols. P4 requires certain additional processing to determine the timestamp to assign to the request. Once a timestamp is assigned and accepted by all the other nodes in the network, the transaction is processed using the P3 protocol. When the originating node determines that a request does not fit into one of the predefined classes, it advances its local clock to some arbitrary future time and uses this as the request's timestamp. The attempt is simply to provide a timestamp beyond that of any transaction currently being processed anywhere in the network. The originating node then broadcasts the P4 request and its timestamp to all the other nodes. If none of the requests a receiving node is processing has a later timestamp, then the P4 request is accepted. If all the nodes accept the P4 request, the originating node can proceed to process the request as if it were simply another P3 request. However, if any node is processing a request with a later timestamp, it rejects the timestamp of the P4 request. If this happens, the originating node restarts the request with an even later timestamp and reissues the P4 request. This procedure for determining the timestamp for a P4 request is the only place in this synchronization procedure where a reject can occur. Only the timestamp, not the request, is being rejected. Also, even in this case the reject is only to the originating node, which can restart the request. The user never receives an indication that the request was rejected.

8–7. Conclusions

This chapter has discussed the update synchronization problem that must be resolved before distributed database management systems can achieve wide acceptability. Although the synchronization or concurrency problem has been adequately solved for the centralized approach, in the distributed environment many approaches are still being developed and tested. This chapter has focused on only four of them. Before any one of them is generally accepted, there must be many more performance analyses to determine the various trade-offs among them. For example, there have been few analyses of the effects of network topology and the degree of data replication on the relative performance of the various synchronization methods. Only with the last approach that was described, using multiple protocols, has there been any analysis of the effects of different types of transactions on the performance of different protocols. For these reasons it is far too early to begin to concentrate on any single synchronization protocol.

Update synchronization is still an issue for researchers and DDBMS software designers but is not yet an issue for the database administrators (DBAs) and should never be an issue for the database users. The user must simply be assured that the synchronization problem has been solved satisfactorily. In some cases this may also be sufficient for the database administrator. In other cases, however, the database administrator in a distributed environment must become more directly involved in the synchronization procedures. The DBA will not have to design and validate synchronization procedures, but he must be able to verify that the level of synchronization a DDBMS provides is sufficient to meet the needs of his organization. The level of synchronization provided and the performance of the DDBMS will be important selection criteria. At least for the foreseeable future, for performance reasons the DBA will probably want to analyze his problem and select the DDBMS that provides the minimum acceptable synchronization level. Although this will initially limit the flexibility of the system, the problem should be only temporary. If DBMS development in the past is any indication of future DDBMSs development, these limitations will gradually be removed as the initially limited DDBMSs are enhanced. At a more direct level, once the DBA has selected a DDBMS, he may then need to identify transaction classes and select the most appropriate data distribution alternative. These design choices are crucial because the appropriate data distribution alternative can simplify the transaction classes and reduce the complexity of the necessary synchronization procedure. This can drastically improve the performance of the DDBMS. To assist the DBA in this design task, the DDBMS vendors must provide a more complete set of database design tools to analyze these various distributed database design options.

Notes

1. CODASYL Systems Committee, *A Framework for Distributed Database Systems: Distributed Alternatives and Generic Architectures,* (New York: Association for Computing Machinery, 1981).

2. D. Cohen and E.M. Rifkin, "Distributed Data Management in Information Systems," Hawaii International Conference on Systems Sciences (January 1981).

3. R.H. Thomas, "A Majority Consensus Approach to Concurrency Control for Multiple Copy Databases," *ACM Trans. on Database Systems* 4, no. 2 (June 1979):180–209.

4. P.A. Berstein, J.B. Rothnie, N. Goodman, and C.A. Papadimitriou, "The Concurrency Control Mechanism in SDD-1: A System for Distributed Databases," *IEEE Trans. Software Engineering* 4, no. 3 (May 1978):154–168.

5. P.A. Berstein, D.W. Shipman, and J.B. Rothnie, "Concurrency Control in a System for Distributed Databases (SDD-1)," *ACM Trans. on Database Systems* 5, no. 1 (March 1980):18–51.

9   Request Decomposition

This chapter discusses request decomposition, the fourth major distributed database management system design issue. (The other three discussed in previous chapters, are data placement, function distribution, and update synchronization.) This chapter is organized into three sections, the first of which discusses one type of request decomposition that is necessary in both centralized and distributed systems. This involves decomposing a high-level, nonprocedural request into a series of low-level, procedural ones. This problem arises in both CODASYL and relational DBMSs. The second section reviews the types of extensions that are necessary in the distributed database environment. The final section identifies some of the major unresolved research issues. These issues must be addressed in order to generalize the current approaches, which were usually developed for very specific situations.

9–1. Request Decomposition in a Centralized DBMS

The need for request decomposition arises in a centralized DBMS whenever a high-level query language is used. The high-level request must be decomposed into a series of low-level requests that the DBMS can process. Although the specific procedure is different, this type of decomposition may be needed by either a CODASYL or a relational system.

This type of decomposition is required by all CODASYL DBMSs that have a high-level query language. The CODASYL data manipulation language is procedural and requires the user to specify how to obtain the desired data—that is, how to navigate through the network data structure. To relieve the user of this burden, a high-level query language is often provided. In this case there must be additional software to decompose the request into a series of actual CODASYL requests that do the navigation. The requests that result from the decomposition are valid DBMS requests, which a user could also issue. They are not internal DBMS operations, such as those that do physical I/O, follow pointer chains, or search inversion tables. This level of decomposition, though important, is not considered in this chapter.

For example, assume a user wants a list of all of the parts that are in a particular product line and have a supplier in Los Angeles. This high-level request is not really a CODASYL request that a CODASYL DBMS could accept. Therefore, additional decomposition software must be provided to take this high-level request and the data definition and generate a series of low-level CODASYL requests that the DBMS could actually execute. All the DBMSs that provide a high-level query language also include special software to perform this function. To answer this high-level user request, a series of low-level subrequests must be issued to the CODASYL DBMS. There are two possible strategies for processing this request. One approach is first to find the proper product-line record or records, then to get a list of all of the parts that are members of the appropriate INCLUDES set. Then, for each part, find its owner in the SUPPLIES set and determine where the supplier is located. The other approach uses the reverse procedure. It first identifies all the suppliers in Los Angeles and then uses the SUPPLIES set to determine the parts they supply. Then, for each part, its owner in the INCLUDES set is checked to see whether the part is a member of the specified product line. In some cases only one of the paths may exist. For example, if it is not possible to go from a part record to its supplier, then the second approach would be the only alternative. If either approach could be used, then the DBMS must have some decision rule to determine which strategy to use. The decision would be based on such factors as which alternative requires the fewest I/Os or which alternative could eliminate the most records the earliest. For example, if there were only ten Los Angeles suppliers and they supplied an average of only 20 parts, but there were 100 product lines each with an average of 200 parts, then the supplier-to-part-to-product-line approach would result in far less processing. The physical organization of the database and the access paths are optimized for certain alternatives depending on the relative frequency of various types of requests.

Similar decomposition procedures may also be needed in a relational DBMS. When the user issues a request based on the nonprocedural relational calculus, the relational system must go through the same type of high- to low-level decomposition to determine how to process the request. (The only exceptions are special purpose database computers in which special hardware is designed to execute high-level relational queries directly.) The main difference is that in the CODASYL example the DBMS was forced to use predefined sets as access paths, whereas the relational DBMS could construct the necessary paths dynamically by joining the appropriate relations. However, even in this case some prior information was needed. The common fields on which various relations could be joined had to be predefined.

Because relational DBMSs can dynamically create access paths, far more decomposition alternatives are possible. This requires more complex decomposition algorithms, which must now solve two problems. First, they must determine what relations can be joined and in what order to produce the desired result. Second, because there can be many different ways to process the request, the algorithms must also select a specific approach to use. Ideally, the optimum approach would be selected. However, in practice it is usually sufficient to find an alternative that simply performs reasonably well. There can be tremendous performance differences among alternatives, up to several orders of magnitude, such as seconds versus hours. Therefore, an algorithm that came within 10 or 15 percent of the optimum would probably be sufficient, especially if it required evaluating far fewer alternatives than an optimizing algorithm.

9–2. Request Decomposition in a Distributed DBMS

The foregoing discussion has assumed a centralized DBMS. This type of high- to low-level decomposition is also required in a distributed environment. Recall that a DDBMS can have three types of requests: local, remote, and compound. Since local and remote requests can both be processed at a single node, the request decomposition algorithms developed for the centralized case can be used with no changes. This algorithm would be used at the point at which the local DBMS would determine the local processing strategy. If the particular DDBMS allowed only local and remote requests, then the centralized decomposition algorithms would be sufficient.

A DDBMS should, however, allow compound requests. For these compound requests the centralized algorithms, though necessary, are not sufficient. A second type of decomposition is also required. Since compound requests cannot be processed directly, they must be decomposed into several simpler subrequests, which a local DBMS can directly process or further decompose. These compound requests must be decomposed because parts of them must be processed at different nodes. In most cases there will be many ways to decompose and process a compound request. Determining how to decompose a request is one of the major functions in selecting a request processing strategy. The NDBMS should do this. If the function is not provided by the NDBMS, then the flexibility and performance of the DDBMS is reduced. Users would only be able to issue local or remote requests. This would force the user or the application program to decompose any compound requests before issuing them to the DDBMS. The application would then issue a series of local or remote requests. The user or the application would have to know how to decompose the original request, as well as the node to which each of the subrequests it generated must be sent. This would force the user or the programmer to know far more about the system than is desirable. Therefore, the existing centralized decomposition algorithms must be enhanced so that compound requests can be decomposed.

Additional factors must be considered in designing an algorithm for decomposing compound requests. The previous section discussed request decomposition in a centralized environment. With a centralized DBMS, communications costs and delays do not complicate the optimization process. In fact, even with remote requests in distributed environment there is little additional complexity, although the communications system does affect the performance. In both these cases the problem is simply to identify the various ways in which the request can be processed and select one of the acceptable approaches. With compound requests the problem becomes more complex because there are far more alternatives to evaluate and the communications factors must also be evaluated.

An objective must be specified against which to evaluate the various decomposition alternatives. The objective usually focuses on one of several possible criteria. First, the objective may be to minimize the response time for the request. This response time includes both processing and communications time. In a lightly loaded system, this criterion may be the most important one. One way to minimize the response time is to decompose the request to allow the maximum amount of parallelism, with different parts of the request being processed at different nodes. This approach would also be subject to the constraint that it minimized the communications time. This is because of the relatively greater time delays in communications than in processing. For example, one would rarely break up a request that could be processed locally and send part of it to another node just so that parallel processing could be used. The time delays caused by the communications would probably be greater than the savings incurred by the parallelism. A more heavily loaded system may have a different objective—to minimize the total processing time for the request. In this case parallelism is sacrificed to minimize the amount of processing.

The processing time for a request can be divided into two parts. A certain amount of time is required to process the request. The amount of total processing time is approximately the same regardless of the number of nodes involved in processing the request. However, some of this time can be overlapped if different nodes are processing the request in parallel. For example, if 10 seconds of total processing time is needed, by overlapping the processing the response time may be reduced to only 4 seconds. A second type of processing time is the overhead processing required for the communications software and consolidation of the results that have been produced independently by several nodes operating in parallel. This overhead processing increases with the number of nodes involved in processing the request. Therefore, in a heavily loaded system that was compute-bound, the objective would be to minimize the total processing time for each request in order to increase the throughput of the system. This would mean minimizing the number of nodes involved in the processing whenever this would reduce the amount of overhead processing. The same decision would be made even if the communications paths rather than the processing were the heavily loaded ones. In this case the number of nodes would be minimized to reduce the amount of communications.

To summarize the two approaches, with the first approach (minimizing the response time) increasing the processing overhead is acceptable as long as it reduces the response time for a request. In the second case (minimizing the total processing time) the overhead processing is minimized to increase the throughput of the system, even if it increases the response time for individual requests.

As with the centralized approach, the selection of a distributed decomposition alternative can be considered as a two-step procedure. The first step is to determine the various alternatives that can be used to process the request. The second step is to use cost and timing equations to evaluate each of the alternatives so that the "best" alternative can be selected. The basic equations are:

$$\text{Minimize (response time or total time)} = f \left(\frac{\text{Processing}}{\text{time}} + \frac{\text{Communications}}{\text{time}} \right)$$

$$\text{Minimize (cost)} = f \left(\frac{\text{Processing}}{\text{costs}} + \frac{\text{Communications}}{\text{costs}} + \frac{\text{Storage}}{\text{costs}} \right)$$

Most of the algorithms, however, do not use this type of explicit two-step procedure because of the tremendous number of possible alternatives. Normally, the two steps are combined into a single step. An initial solution or decomposition alternative is selected and evaluated, based on the evaluation criteria specified in the design. Then a slightly different alternative is selected and evaluated. If the new alternative results in an improvement, then it becomes the baseline against which subsequent alternatives are compared. If it does not provide an improvement, then another variation is selected, evaluated, and compared against the baseline. The algorithm stops when it cannot find a more effective way to decompose the request or when a certain number of attempts have resulted in a minimal improvement. This type of algorithm is a hill-climbing optimization procedure. It finds a local optimum, but there is no guarantee that it will find a global optimum.

9–3. Future Issues

The two previous sections have discussed centralized and distributed request decomposition. This section identifies several key issues that must be addressed in the future. Almost all the current research in the distributed area has been directed at solving the decomposition problem for a specific system, in most cases with a relatively simple extension of the centralized algorithms. Therefore, for other significantly different types of DDBMSs, different methods may be more appropriate. For example, the cost models used to evaluate the various decomposition alternatives make certain simplifying assumptions. In some cases these assumptions are acceptable, but with significantly different system architectures, they may be inappropriate. This section identifies several of the key areas in which different assumptions may lead to different algorithms.

Nature of the Problem

So far, the decomposition algorithms have involved only a single criterion or objective. Since there are several possible criteria that could be used, the decomposition could be defined as a bicriteria problem, rather than as a simple optimization problem. This bicriteria approach has been used in some of the data placement studies, where several design decisions (for example, data placement and storage allocation to the various nodes) were made jointly. Possible combinations involve selecting a decomposition algorithm jointly with a network topology, data placement or node processing, and storage capacity.

Network Topology

Most of the research has assumed a specific network topology. There have not been any detailed studies evaluating the performance of various decomposition algorithms for a variety of topologies. Recall that the two possible objectives of request decomposition are to minimize the response time or the total time. These objectives affect the amount of communications and parallel processing. The trade-off is that additional communications are required to initiate the processing at various nodes and to obtain the results once the processing has been completed. The network topology can facilitate or hinder this communication. For example, with a star topology the central node can become a major communications bottleneck. Therefore, for this type of network topology minimizing the communications may be more important than obtaining additional parallelism. On the other hand, with a completely interconnected topology communications would be less of a problem. Therefore, in this case the more important objective could be to maximize the amount of parallelism rather than to minimize the communications. Regardless of the network topology, the technology used in the various communications links can affect the performance of various decomposition algorithms.

Communications Technology

Communications technology is reflected in the bandwidth and costs of the communications links. These two factors determine the cost-performance of the system. This cost-performance is a part of the cost model used by the decomposition algorithm to evaluate the various alternatives. A slow, low-bandwidth communications path increases the importance of minimizing the amount of communications through the network, whereas a very high bandwidth path could reduce the importance of this objective. Another factor is that most of the cost models assume a single type of communications technology throughout the network. Furthermore, they often assume that the costs of communications are independent of the length of the path. Finally, a key assumption that is always made is that communications costs and delays are far greater than processing costs and time. This places a high priority on minimizing the amount of communications. If the relative performance of communications and processing were more balanced, the trade-off between the objectives of minimizing communications and maximizing processing parallelism would be different. In an extreme case, if communications were very fast and cheap, and processing relatively slow (for example, a local network of microcomputers linked with a fiber optics loop). then the trade-off priority would be to trade processing for communications.

Data Placement

In the chapter on data placement it was pointed out that there are several ways to define the placement problem by using a single objective or several joint or related objectives. Request decomposition and data placement are related issues, but so far this interrelationship has not been adequately researched. Most of the data placement studies have assumed either local or remote requests. Except for the issue of update synchronization, data placement studies have not addressed the question of how to decompose compound requests and how data placement alternatives affect the decomposition algorithms. Multiple copies of the data create complications for update synchronization, but they also allow more possibilities for parallelism in request processing.

Enhancements in the data placement studies are needed because one of their major assumptions breaks down when request decomposition is required. The files or fragments of data that are being placed are assumed to be independent of each other. This is clearly not the case with compound requests. Replicated data are obviously related because of the update synchronization problem. Data fragments are also potentially related whenever there is a common join field or, in the CODASYL terminology, whenever set membership spans nodes or when owner records and member records of a set are placed at different nodes. Placing data that are logically related and jointly referenced at the same node reduces the complexity of the requests. It can reduce what would have been a compound request to a local or a remote request. On the other hand, this type of placement minimizes the opportunity for parallel processing

parts of the same request. This type of trade-off relating data placement procedures and decomposition algorithms has not yet been done.

Single or Multiple Requests

Another key assumption in request decomposition algorithms is that the processing for a request is done independently of any other requests in the system.
At any particular time this may not result in the optimal processing time. For
example, if the node at which the initial local processing was to be done was
saturated, a faster response time might be possible if the initial processing were
done at another node. Similarly, if part of a request must be processed at each
of several nodes, but some of the processing could be arbitrarily assigned to
any one of them, then the current load at each node should be considered. To
take this type of request interaction into account requires either dynamically
adjusting the decomposition algorithm or dynamically updating the data used
to evaluate the various alternatives. The required system monitoring would add
complexity to the algorithm. However, there are already many parts of the
operating system that make these types of adjustments. Disk scheduling algorithms almost always consider this type of interaction.

9–4. Summary

This chapter began by reviewing request decomposition in a centralized DBMS.
This high-level to low-level request decomposition exists in both a centralized
and a distributed environment. The additional complexity caused by remote and
compound requests were discussed in section 9–2, which also described two
approaches to request decomposition. One approach minimizes the response
time, whereas the other tries to minimize the total processing time. Section 9–3
identified several additional factors that should be considering in developing
and evaluating request decomposition algorithms. These include the nature of
the problem, the network topology, the communications technology, the data
placement, and the optimization of a set of requests rather than a single request.

10 Conclusion

This concluding chapter consists of three sections. The first section provides a summary of the major concepts discussed in the book. The second briefly discusses some of the organizational and administrative issues that will arise and must be resolved when an organization begins to move into a distributed database environment. The third section reviews some of the major unresolved technical issues in the distributed database area and makes some projections about future developments.

10–1. Summary

This book provides an introduction to the concepts of distributed database management, particularly as they have been developed by the CODASYL Systems Committee. It begins by identifying the four basic objectives of database management: ease of use, evolvability, integrity, and data security. It then discusses database management as it currently exists in a centralized environment. The next topic is the basic concepts of data communications and distributed processing in general. The basic organizational and technical objectives of distributed processing are also identified. Most of these considerations also apply directly to distributed database management. The organizational objectives involved improved responsiveness, especially in the application development area, and improved control. The technical objectives included faster access, lower costs, greater reliability and improved modular growth.

The discussion of the actual components and functions of distributed database management began in chapter 5. Four new network-related components must be added to a centralized DBMS to allow it to operate in a distributed environment. The components include the network access process (NAP), the network description, the network data directory (NDD), and the network database management system (NDBMS). The NAP provides the communications facilities to link a node to the network. It uses the network description to determine how to route messages, which may be either user requests or data responses. The NDD specifies how the data are distributed. It is used by the NDBMS to locate data in the network and to determine a network-wide strategy for processing a request. Additional functions of the NDBMS include providing the interface between the user and the system (either the local DBMS or the

143

rest of the network), providing network-wide backup and recovery procedures, and translating between systems in a heterogeneous distributed system.

To reemphasize the point, these new components provide one way of implementing a DDBMS. If they are used, then most of the parts of current centralized DBMSs can remain virtually unchanged, with all the new functions placed in the new components. However, to do this assumes certain packaging decisions about how the various DDBMS functions are clustered. They need not be so clustered in every case. The intention in discussing these new components in this way is to provide a more specific context in which to illustrate the necessary new functions that are required by a DDBMS.

Chapter 7 describes each of the functions (both new and old) that are required to process requests in a DDBMS. It also specifies how these functions can be distributed. Based on various function distribution alternatives, several node configurations are identified. These configurations include a complete node, a database computer node, and several minimal node configurations.

Various data distribution options, including centralized, replicated, partitioned, and hybrid, are described; and the advantages and problems of each option are listed. Unresolved issues in both data placement and function placement are also described.

The update synchronization problem is described, and four specific solutions are discussed, along with the conditions under which each would be appropriate. The four alternatives are global locking, dominant copy, majority consensus, and variable protocols.

There is also a discussion of request decomposition procedures, which are necessary for two reasons. The first type of decomposition, which also exists in a centralized DBMS, is done to convert high-level, user-oriented requests into a series of low-level requests that the DBMS can execute. The second type, unique to distributed systems, is done to allow the user to issue requests that are independent of how the database is distributed. The NDBMS uses its knowledge of how the database is distributed to decompose compound requests into a series of local and remote requests that individual local DBMSs can then execute.

10–2. Administrative Issues

No discussion of database management or distributed database management would be complete without some consideration of the organizational and administrative issues. With a centralized DBMS two sets of functions have emerged. At the technical level there are the functions of database administration; at a higher, organizational level, there is a similar data administration function.

The functions of *database administration* include:

1. defining the database
2. controlling access to the database
3. providing tools to increase the availability of the data
4. providing backup and recovery procedures

   The database administrator (DBA) may be either an individual or an entire department, depending on the size of the organization and its database. The DBA defines the database, including the record types, the fields within each type, the sets relating the various record types, and the access paths by which they are processed. Ideally, this database design is the result of a top-down analysis of the information requirements of the entire organization, although this analysis may be done on a function-by-function basis as new applications are developed and integrated into the database. The DBA must also define the subschemas that allow users or applications to access and use specific parts of the database. Because an organization's database requirements change over time, the DBA sometimes must modify or redefine the database structure to meet these new needs, while ensuring that current users who do not need the redefinition can continue to access and use the database.

   The DBA also controls access to the database by directly specifying to the DBMS which users have access to which parts of the database to do which operations. In some cases the DBA actually makes the decision about who has access to what, but in many cases he simply implements access control decisions made by others—for example, users who have integrated their data into the database. Sometimes the access control methods provided by the DBMS are not sufficient to meet an organization's requirements. In these cases the DBA must write additional database procedures to provide the necessary enhanced access control procedures.

   The third function of the DBA is to provide the necessary tools to make the database readily available to the authorized users. These tools may include high-level query languages, report writers, and predefined transactions. The DBA must also monitor the performance of the DBMS and, when necessary, reorganize the database to improve its performance. A reorganization of the database, unlike restructuring, does not change the database definition but simply adjusts the physical storage of the database to eliminate minor inefficiencies that have developed because of add and delete operations.

   Finally, the DBA is responsible for defining and implementing the necessary backup and recovery procedures. Backup procedures may include periodic dumps of the database, a transaction log, and an audit trail of before and/or after images for every change to the database. Recovery procedures are necessary either to roll back or to bring forward the database when an error has occurred. The appropriate combination of backup and recovery procedures is selected by making trade-offs between their costs and time, on the one hand, and, on the other, the value of the data and how long they can safely remain unavailable during a recovery procedure. The result of these trade-offs may be that different parts of the database are protected by different backup and recovery procedures.

At a higher organizational level another function, *data administration*, is beginning to emerge. This function focuses on the data management requirements for the entire organization, regardless of whether the data are actually in a database. The database administration function, though recognized earlier, is really only a subset of the data administration function. For each database administration function there is a corresponding, but broader, data administration function. For example, instead of just defining the database, the data administrator must define the data requirements of the entire organization. This can include what data are collected, when they are collected, by whom, on what forms, how long they are retained, and whether or not they are entered into the database. The data administrator must also specify the access and security controls to be placed on the data and how various privacy regulations are to be met. Although the data administration functions are broader and more encompassing, they frequently emerge from the more limited database administration functions. An organization has only one data administrator or department regardless of its size and the number of database administrators it has.

In current centralized systems there is a single database administrator for each database or, occasionally, for each site (if there are several databases at a single site). A distributed system has many nodes, however, and the database administration function can be much more complicated, depending on how the system developed. There are three ways in which an organization may develop a distributed system. The first approach is to go directly to a distributed system when a new system or application is initially being developed. The second approach is to take a system that is currently centralized and begin to distribute certain functions out to local nodes. The third approach is to add a communications system and begin to link several currently independent nodes into a distributed system. In either of the first two cases, the database administration function may be relatively easy. It was organized and designed centrally. Now, as necessary or desirable, some of its functions can be gradually distributed out to the various nodes.

When the DDBMS comes about as a result of merging several previously independent nodes, the database administration function results in many more organizational problems. Presumably, each of these independent nodes already has a database administrator. When they were independent, each of these database administrators provide centralized control and performed the database administration functions described earlier for their own nodes. In a distributed system, however, the actions of these independent database administrators must be coordinated. This coordination is complicated by the geographic dispersion of both the users of each node and the database administrators who represent them. Trying to provide some coordination mechanism, such as data definition and programming standards, can create serious organizational problems. Furthermore, the traditional database administration functions with which everyone is familiar are complicated by the distributed environment.

For example, the data definition function is complicated because the data placement issue must be resolved. If part of the data is to be replicated, there must be an agreement on how often the copies must be updated. Some users may want the copies closely synchronized, whereas others may be satisfied with overnight updating as long as there is a current copy of the data somewhere in the system. The latter alternative raises the issue of where to store the dominant copy. Also, if part of the data is replicated, which users have the primary responsibility for the data and the strongest incentive to correct any errors and maintain data quality? If the database is partitioned, how is it partitioned and where is each part stored? Since different placement decisions can have a serious impact on a user's performance, it may be very difficult for several "semi-independent" database administrators to make these decisions. These decisions, however, may be easier in the first two approaches in which the database administration function began and remained centralized.

Similar problems arise with the other database administration functions. For example, when a user or a local database administrator has his data replicated, he may perceive a loss of control. Depending on the quality of the access controls in the network, he may be concerned that the security and integrity of the data can be compromised. Determining a common set of backup and recovery procedures is also more complicated when different users have different requirements.

The important point is that most of these issues are organizational rather than technical ones. Even if all the remaining technical problems described in the next section were solved, these organizational problems would still remain. There is a strong similarity between this problem and the one that was faced twenty years ago in data processing. At that time hardware was the critical bottleneck. Gradually, that bottleneck was eliminated, and now everyone seems to agree that software development is the critical bottleneck. However, this change was recognized very late, and there was much misplaced effort expended by many people in trying to solve the wrong problem. A similar situation seems to be developing today in the distributed processing and distributed database areas. Software development is still the immediate problem for distributed systems, but it is rapidly being resolved. When these software bottlenecks are resolved, the organizational issues will become the critical bottleneck in designing and implementing distributed systems. Unfortunately, many of the organizational issues that must be resolved to remove this next bottleneck are not yet being addressed, and often they are not even being recognized by many of the people now working in the distributed database area.

10–3. Future Directions

This concluding section attempts to provide some indications of the future direction of distributed database management activity and of the types of facilities that will begin to emerge. Currently, there are two types of DDBMSs. First, there are a few systems with a fairly extensive set of capabilities. However, these systems are operational only in very restricted research and development environments. They currently do not have the performance or, in some cases, the reliability of commercially viable products. In some cases their algorithms have been designed but are still being prototyped and tuned. Some of these systems may eventually become commercial products, but others may never become commercially viable. They may simply remain prototypes and testbeds to help understand the problems and study some of the approaches that may later be used in commercial DDBMSs.

The second type of DDBMSs available today are those that are outgrowths of currently available commercial centralized DBMSs. As yet, these systems provide relatively limited distributed capabilities, essentially permitting only local and remote requests. Over time these systems will be enhanced to provide a more complete set of the functions and capabilities discussed in the previous chapters. Relational systems and those that include high-level query languages will be enhanced. Database management systems that do not meet one of these requirements will either add a high-level query language or will begin to decline in popularity. They will be locked out of the two major areas of future database management systems development—distributed database management and database computers.

Most current database management systems will probably develop a fairly standard migration path from a centralized to a distributed system. This will happen for competitive reasons and because of the direction in which software technology is developing. Initially, there will be the capability to define the database and spread it over several nodes, but without replication. The update synchronization problem will be avoided, rather than solved, at this point. This approach will then allow local and remote requests. Complex request processing strategies will also be avoided for the time being. All that the system will be required to do will be to determine the node to which to send the remote request. Some DDBMSs already allow users to issue remote requests without having to know where the data are located or even whether the request is local or remote.

The next step will probably be to add a very limited form of replication. This will involve the concept of a snapshot. A snapshot is a copy of a part of the database. The DDBMS will know where these snapshots are and can use them for local retrievals; in some cases they may also be used by other nodes for remote retrievals. The key characteristic of the snapshot, however, is that it is as of a certain point in time. The DDBMS will not automatically update and maintain the snapshot. Therefore, over a period of time the snapshot will become out of date and will have to be created again. This represents an intermediate step in the evolution of DDBMSs. It provides a limited form of replication and improves the performance of retrievals as long as the very latest data are not essential. At the same time it can be provided without incurring the major performance penalties involved in update synchronization. Obviously, this approach will not meet the needs of all applications.

Eventually, there will be commercially viable DDBMSs that permit replicated and hybrid data distribution alternatives. Initially, the emphasis of these DDBMSs will be on their more complete functionality; but later versions will begin to provide a competitive performance. The increasing functionality will permit these systems to allow more complex types of compound requests. In applications developed for earlier versions of these DDBMSs, before they permitted compound requests, the programmer or user had to decompose any such requests into an equivalent series of local and remote requests. These applications, using only local and remote requests, will still be able to run on the later enhanced versions of the DDBMSs.

Another development that must occur with the widespread introduction and acceptance of distributed database management is the development of improved database design tools. The design of a centralized database is relatively complex, but the design of a distributed database is much more complex. It has all the complexity of the centralized database, plus the added complexity of data placement decisions, update synchronization, and request decomposition. There is also the problem of designing the communications system. The DBA must be provided with additional design tools to help him solve these problems. These tools will be of two types. Analytical tools will help him evaluate a large number of possible alternative designs and focus on a few of the best designs. Further simulation analysis with the other set of tools will permit a more precise analysis of these potential designs and the fine tuning of the exact design that is selected.

Two types of research are still needed in the area of distributed database management. The first—the analysis of a single aspect, such as data placement—has already been done fairly extensively. Other well-covered facets are communications systems, update synchronization, and request decomposition. Some additional work is needed in a few areas. Most of this type of work had one focus and assumed that everything else was held constant. Initially, this assumption was acceptable and probably even necessary in developing a basic understanding of each of these facets. However, a second type of research is now needed. This must focus on the combined effects and interactions between these aspects. For example, there is a strong interaction between data placement and update synchronization. Given a specific data placement and a set of requests, one can calculate the communications requirements of the system. For the update requests, however, these communications requirements are very different depending on how the updates are synchronized. Therefore, these two decisions should really be made jointly. There are similar interactions between data placement and request decomposition because when the data placement is changed, the same request can change from a local to a remote request or from a remote to a compound request. These interactions must be better understood and modeled to provide the types of design and development tools mentioned earlier. This research and the resulting design tools will aid both the designers who must develop the DDBMSs and the DBAs who must select them and design the databases that they will manage.

There is one last area in which there will probably be intensive distributed database activity in the immediate future. It involves local networks. So far, most of the work in distributed database management has concentrated on networks that were widely dispersed and that used relatively conventional communications technologies. In the last two or three years there has been intense activity in local networks, but this activity has not yet affected the database and distributed database area. This will change very soon because the communications technologies being used to implement these local networks are very different from those technologies used for geographically dispersed systems. These differences will lead to several significantly different approaches to various database and distributed database problems.

In summary, although the past several years have seen much activity in the distributed database management area, very limited DDBMSs are just now beginning to emerge in the commercial environment. The next few years will see far more changes and developments. Finally, the benefits and improved versatility promised by DDBMS will at last begin to reach the marketplace.

Bibliography

This book, intended as an introduction to and overview of distributed database management systems, has covered many issues. Much more could be said about any one of these areas. For example, an entire book could be written about update synchronization, request decomposition, or data placement. This bibliography, subdivided by major area, is intended to assist those readers who need more detailed information on specific areas.

Conference papers provide the most current material on most of these areas. An attempt has been made to concentrate on those papers and conference proceedings that should be widely available. There are several conferences that focus specifically on the issues and areas addressed in this book. The reader who wants to stay current on the distributed database area should make it a practice to review the proceedings of each of these conferences in order to find the latest papers on his or her particular interests. These conferences include the Berkeley Workshop on Distributed Data Management and Computer Networks, the International Conference on Very Large Data Bases (VLDB), and the ACM International Conference on the Management of Data.

There are also several general conferences that include some papers in the database, distributed processing, and the distributed database areas. These conferences include the AFIPS National Computer Conference, the ACM Annual Conference, the IEEE Fall and Spring COMPCONs, and the IEEE Computer Software and Applications Conference.

Database Management Systems (General)

Fry, J.P., and E.H. Sibley. "Evolution of Data Base Management Systems." *Computing Surveys* 8, no. 1 (March 1976):7–42.
Martin, J. *Computer Data-Base Organization*. Englewood Cliffs, N.J.: Prentice-Hall, 1975.
———. *Principles of Data-Base Management*. Englewood Cliffs, N.J.: Prentice-Hall, 1976.
Thurber, K.J., and P.C. Patton. *Data Structures and Computer Architecture: Design Issues at the Hardware/Software Interface*. Lexington, Mass.: Lexington Books, D.C. Heath and Company, 1977.

Database Management Systems (Relational)

Astraham, M.M., et al. "System R: Relational Approach to Database Management." *ACM Trans. on Database Systems* 1, no. 2 (June 1976):97–137.

Codd, E.F. "A Relational Model of Data for Large Shared Data Banks." *Comm. ACM* 13, no. 6 (June 1970):377–387.

———. "Extending the Database Relational Model to Capture More Meaning." *ACM Trans. Database Systems* 4, no. 4 (December 1979):397–434.

Kim, W. "Relational Database Systems." *ACM Trans. Database Systems* 11, no. 3 (September 1979):185–212.

Lozinskii, E. "Construction of Relations in Relational Databases." *ACM Trans. Database Systems* 5, no. 2 (June 1980):208–224.

Schmid, H.A., and P.A. Bernstein. "A Multi-level Architecture for Relational Database Systems." *Proc. VLDB* (September 1975):202–226.

Data Base Computers

Bray, O.H. "Data Base Computers: A New Generation of Backend Storage Subsystems." *Proc. Hawaii International Conference on System Sciences* (January 1981).

Bray, O.H., and H.A. Freeman. *Data Base Computers*. Lexington, Mass.: Lexington Books, D.C. Heath and Company, 1979.

Canaday, R.N., R.D. Harrison, E.C. Ivie, J.C. Ryder, and L.A. Wehr. "A Back-end Computer for Data Base Management." *Communications of ACM* 17, no. 10 (October 1974):575–582.

Lowenthal, E.I. "A Survey—The Application of Data Base Management Systems." *Proc. VLDB* (October 1977):85–92.

Marill, T., and D.H. Stern. "The Datacomputer: A Network Data Utility." *Proc. NCC 1975*, pp. 389–395.

Data Communications

Abrams, M., R.P. Blanc, and I.W. Cotton. *Computer Networks: A Tutorial* Long Beach, Calif.: IEEE Computer Society, 1980.

Abramson, N., and F. Kuo, eds. *Computer Communications Networks*. Englewood Cliffs, N.J.: Prentice-Hall, 1973.

Anderson, G.A., and E.D. Jensen. "Computer Interconnection: Taxonomy, Characteristics and Examples." *Computing Surveys* 7, no. 4 (December 1975):197–214.

Hollis, L.L. "Open Systems Inter-Connection Upper Layers Activity." *Proc. COMPCON80* (Fall 1980):558–563.

Jardins, R. des. "Overview and Status of the ISO/ANSI Reference Model of Open Systems Interconnection." *Proc. COMPCON80* (Fall 1980):553–557.

Kimbleton, S.R., and G.M. Schneider. "Computer Communications Networks:

Approaches, Objectives and Performance Considerations." *Computing Surveys* 7, no. 3 (September 1975):129–173.

Larson, R.E. *Tutorial: Distributed Control*. Long Beach, Calif.: IEEE Computer Society, 1979.

Liebowitz, B.H., and J.H. Carson. *Distributed Processing*, 2nd ed. Long Beach, Calif.: IEEE Computer Society, 1978.

Martin, J. *Systems Analysis for Data Transmission*. Englewood Cliffs, N.J.: Prentice-Hall, 1972.

———. *Telecommunications and the Computer*, 2nd ed. Englewood Cliffs, N.J.: Prentice-Hall, 1976.

———. *Communications Satellite Systems*. Englewood Cliffs, N.J.: Prentice-Hall, 1978.

———. *Computer Networks and Distributed Processing: Software, Techniques and Architecture*. Englewood Cliffs, N.J.: Prentice-Hall, 1981.

McGovern, J.P., and D. Basu. "Middle Layers of Open Systems Interconnections: Session and Transport." *Proc. COMPCON80* (Fall 1980):564–571.

Thurber, K.J. *Tutorial: Distributed Processor Communication Architecture*. Long Beach, Calif.: IEEE Computer Society, 1979.

———. *Tutorial: A Pragmatic View of Distributed Processing Systems*. Long Beach, Calif.: IEEE Computer Society, 1980.

———. "An Assessment of the Status of Network Architecture." *Proc. COMPCON80* (Fall 1980):87–94.

Thurber, K.J., and H.A. Freeman. *Tutorial: Local Computer Network Architecture*. Long Beach, Calif.: IEEE Computer Society, 1980.

Thurber, K.J., and G.M. Masson. *Distributed Processor Communication Architecture*. Lexington, Mass.: Lexington Books, 1979.

White, G.W. "Lower Layers of Open Systems Interconnection Architecture: Network, Data Link and Physical Layers." *Proc. COMPCON80* (Fall 1980):572–576.

Distributed Database Management Systems (General)

Aschim, F. "Data Base Networks—An Overview." *Management Informatics* 3, no. 1 (1974):13–28.

Booth, G.M. "Distributed Information Systems." *Proc. NCC 1976* pp. 789–794.

Champine, G.A. "Six Approaches to Distributed Databases." *Datamation* 23, no. 5:69–72.

Chu, W.W., and P.P. Chen. *Tutorial: Centralized and Distributed Data Base Systems*. Long Beach, Calif.: IEEE Computer Society, 1979.

CODASYL Systems Committee. "Distributed Data Base Technology: An Interim Report of the CODASYL Systems Commitee." *Proc. NCC 1978,* pp. 909–918.

———. *A Framework for Distributed Database Systems: Distributed Alternatives and Generic Architectures.* New York, N.Y.: Association for Computing Machinery, 1981.

Cohen, D., and E.M. Rifkin. "Distributed Data Management in Information Systems." *Proc. Hawaii International Conference on System Sciences* (January 1981):589–597.

Davenport, R.A. "Distributed or Centralized Data Base." *Computer Journal* 21, no. 1 (February 1978):7–13.

———. "Distributed Database Technology—A Survey." *Computer Networks* 2, no. 3 (July 1978).

Deppe, M.E., and J.P. Fry. "Distributed Data Bases—A Summary of Research." *Computer Networks* 1, no. 2 (1976):130–138.

Epstein, R., and M. Stonebraker. "Analysis of Distributed Data Base Processing Strategies." *Proc. VLDB* (October 1980):92–101.

Larson, J.A., and T.B. Wilson. "Data Architectures for Distributed Data Bases." *Proc. COMPCON80* (Fall 1980):378–382.

Mager, P.S. "Alternative Architectures for Distributed Data Sharing: Functional Issues." *Proc. COMPCON80* (Fall 1980):371–377.

Manning, E., and R. Peebles. "Systems Architecture for Distributed Data Management." *Computer* 11, no. 1 (January 1978):40–47.

Maryansky, F.J. "A Survey of Developments in Distributed Data Base Management Systems." *Computer* 11, no. 2 (February 1978):28–38.

Peebles, R., and E. Manning. "A Computer Architecture for Large (Distributed) Data Bases." *Proc. VLDB* (September 1976).

Ramamoorthy, C.V. "Architectural Issues in Distributed Data Base Systems." *Proc. VLDB* (October 1977).

Ramamoorthy, C.V., and B.W. Wah, "Data Management in Distributed Data Bases." *Proc. NCC 1979,* pp. 667–680.

Rothnie, J.B., Jr., P.A. Bernstein, and D.W. Shipman. *Tutorial: Distributed Data Base Management.* Long Beach, Calif.: IEEE Computer Society, 1978.

Rothnie, J., and N. Goodman. "A Survey of Research and Development in Distributed Database Management. *Proc. VLDB* (1977).

Tripathi, A.R., E.T. Upchurch, and J.C. Brown. "An Overview of Research Directions in Distributed Processing." *Proc. COMPCON80* (Fall 1980):333–340.

Distributed Database Management Systems and Distributed Processing (Design Methods)

Bray, O.H. "Distributed Database Design Considerations." *Computer Networks: Trends and Applications* (1976).

Dawson, J.L. "A User Demand Model for Distributed Database Design." *Proc. COMPCON80* (Fall 1980):211–216.

Fisher, P.S., P. Hollist, and J. Solnim. "A Design Methodology for Distributed Data Bases." *Proc. COMPCON80* (Fall 1980):199–202.

Hebalkar, P.G., and C. Tung. "Logical Design Considerations for Distributed Database Systems." *Proc. IEEE Computer Software and Applications Conference* (November 1977):562–578.

Heinselman, R.C. "System Design Selection for Distributed Data Systems." *Proc. COMPCON80* (Fall 1980):203–210.

Hevner, A.R., and G.M. Schneider. "An Integrated Design System for Distributed Database Networks." *Proc. COMPCON80* (Fall 1980):459–465.

Kennedy, S.R. The Use of Access Frequencies in Data Base Organization. Ph.D. diss., Cornell University, 1973.

Kunii, T.L., and H.S. Kunii. "Design Criteria for Distributed Data Base Systems." *Proc. VLDB* (October 1977):93–104.

Levin, K.D. "Organizing Distributed Data Bases in Computer Networks." Ph.D. diss., University of Pennsylvania, 1974.

Levin, K.D., and H.L. Morgan. "Optimizing Distributed Data Bases—A Framework for Research." *Proc. NCC 1975*, pp. 473–478.

Loomis, M.E.S. "Data Base Design: Object Distribution and Resource-Constrained Task Scheduling." Ph.D. diss., University of California at Los Angeles, 1975.

Mahmoud, S.A., J.S. Riordon, and K.C. Toth. "Design of a Distributed Data Base File Manager for a Mini-Computer Network." *Proc. IEEE Computer Software and Applications Conference* (November 1977):822–828.

Nahouraii, E., A.F. Cardenas, and O. Brooks. "An Approach to Data Communication between Different Generalized DBMS." *Proc. VLDB* (September 1976).

Palmer, D., and M. Mariani. *Tutorial: Distributed Systems Design.* Long Beach, Calif.: IEEE Computer Society, 1979.

Pelagotti, G., and F.A. Schreiber. "Evaluation of Transmission Requirements in Distributed Database Access." *Proc. ACM International Conference on Management of Data* (May 1979):102–108.

Data Placement

Casey, G. "Allocation of Copies of a File in an Information Network." *Proc. NCC 1972*, pp. 617–625.

Chu, W.W. "Optimal File Allocation in a Multiple Computer System." *IEEE Trans. on Computers* 18, no. 10 (October 1969):885–889.

———. "Performance of File Directory Systems for Databases in Star and Distributed Networks." *Proc. NCC 1976*, pp. 577–587.

Chu, W.W., and E. Nahouraii. "File Directory Design Considerations for Distributed Data Bases." *Proc. VLDB* (September 1975):543–545.

Eswaran, K.P. "Placement of Records in a File and File Allocation in a Computer Network." *Information Processing* 74 (1974):304–307.

Lam, K., and C.T. Yu. "An Approximation Algorithm for a File-Allocation Problem in a Hierarchical Distributed System." *Proc. ACM International Conference on the Management of Data* (May 1980):125–132.

Mahmoud, S., and J.S. Riordon. "Optimal Allocation of Resources in Distributed Information Networks." *ACM Trans. on Database Systems* 1, no. 1 (March 1976):66–78.

Matsushita, Y., et al. "Cost Evaluation of Directory Management Schemes for Distributed Database Systems." *Proc. ACM International Conference on the Management of Data* (May 1980):117–124.

Whitney, V.K.M. "A Study of Optimal File Assignment and Communication Network Configuration." Ph.D. diss., University of Michigan, 1970.

Update Synchronization

Bayer, R., H. Heller, and A. Reisner. "Parallelism and Recovery in Database Systems." *ACM Trans. Database Systems* 5, no. 2 (June 1980):139–156.

Bernstein, P.A., and N. Goodman. "Approaches to Concurrency Control in Distributed Database Systems." *Proc. NCC 1979*, pp. 813–820.

Bernstein, P.A., J.B. Rothnie, N. Goodman, and C.A. Papadimitriou. "The Concurrency Control Mechanism in SDD-1: A System for Distributed Databases." *IEEE Trans. Software Engineering* 4, no. 3 (May 1978):154–168.

Bernstein, P.A., and D.W. Shipman. "The Correctness of Concurrency Control Mechanisms in a System for Distributed Databases (SDD-1)." *ACM Trans. on Database Systems* 5, no. 1 (March 1980):52–68.

Bernstein, P.A., D.W. Shipman, and J.B. Rothnie, Jr. "Concurrency Control in a System for Distributed Databases (SDD-1)." *ACM Trans. on Database Systems* 5, no. 1 (March 1980):18–51.

Bernstein, P.A., D.W. Shipman, and W.S. Wong. "Formal Aspects of Serializability in Database Concurrency Control." *IEEE Trans. Software Engineering* 5, no. 3 (May 1979):203–215.

Cheng, W.K., and G.G. Belford. "Analysis of Update Synchronization Schemes in Distributed Databases." *Proc. COMPCON80* (Fall 1980):450–455.

Chu, W.W., and G. Ohlmacher. "Avoiding Deadlock in Distributed Data Bases." *Proc. ACM National Conference* (1974):156–160.

Ellis, C. "A Robust Algorithm for Updating Duplicate Data Bases." *Proc. Berkeley Workshop on Distributed Data Management and Computer Networks* (May 1977).

Eswaran, K.P., J.N. Gray, R.A. Lorie, and I.L. Traiger. "The Notions of Consistency and Predicate Locks in a Database System." *Comm. ACM* 19, no. 11 (November 1976):624–633.

Garcia-Molina, H. "Reliability Issues for Completely Replicated Distributed Databases." *Proc. COMPCON80* (Fall 1980):442–449.

Gelenbe, E., K. Sevcik. "Analysis of Update Synchronization for Multiple Copy Data Bases." *Proc. Berkeley Workshop on Distributed Data Management and Computer Networks* (August 1978).

Gray, J.N., R. A. Lorie, and G.R. Putzolu. "Granularity of Locks and Degrees of Consistency in a Shared Database." *Proc. VLDB* (September 1975):428–451.

King, P.F., and A.J. Collmeyer. "Database Sharing—An Efficient Method for Supporting Concurrent Processes." *Proc. NCC 1973,* pp. 271–275.

Kohler, W.H. "Overview of Synchronization and Recovery Problems in Distributed Databases." *Proc. COMPCON80* (Fall 1980):433–441.

Lamport, L. "Time, Clocks and Ordering of Events in a Distributed System." *Comm. ACM* 21, no. 7 (July 1978):558–565.

Lee, C., R. Shastri, and R. Metzger. "Distributed Control Schemes for Multiple-Copies Files Access in a Network Environment." *Proc. IEEE Computer Software and Applications Conference* (November 1977).

Lorie, R.A. "Physical Integrity in a Large Segmented Database." *ACM Trans. Database Systems* 2, no. 1 (March 1977):91–104.

Menasce, D.A., G.J. Pope, and R.R. Muntz. "A Locking Protocol for Resource Coordination in Distributed Databases." *ACM Trans. Database Systems* 5, no. 2 (June 1980):103–138.

Ries, D.R., and M. Stonebraker. "Effects of Locking Granularity in a Database Management System." *ACM Trans. Database Systems* (September 1977):233–246.

Rosenkrantz, D.J., R.D. Sterns, and P.M. Lewis. "System Level Concurrency Control for Distributed Database Systems." *ACM Trans. Database Systems* 3, no. 2 (June 1978):178–198.

Shapiro, R., and R. Millstein. "Failure Recovery in a Distributed Data Base System." *Proc. COMPCON 78* (Spring 1978).

Stonebraker, M. "Concurrency Control and Consistency of Multiple Copies of Data in Distributed INGRES." *Trans. Software Engineering* 5, no. 3 (May 1979):203–215.

Thomas, R.H. "A Majority Consensus Approach to Concurrency Control for Multiple Copy Databases." *ACM Trans. Database Systems* 4, no. 2 (June 1979):180–209.

Verhofstad, J.S.M. "Recovery Techniques for Database Systems." *ACM Computing Surveys* 10, no. 2 (June 1978):167–196.

Request Decomposition

Aho, A.V., U. Sagiv, and J.D. Ullman. "Efficient Optimization of a Class of Relational Expressions." *ACM Trans. Database Systems* 4, no. 4 (December 1979):435–454.

Birss, E.W., and J.P. Fry. "Generalized Software for Translating Data." *Proc. NCC 1976*, pp. 889–897.

Chu, W., and P. Hurley. "A Model for Optimal Query Processing for Distributed Data Bases." *Proc. COMCON 79* (Spring 1979):116–122.

Epstein, R., M. Stonebraker, and E. Wong. "Distributed Query Processing in a Relational Data Base System." *Proc. ACM International Conference on Management of Data* (May 1978):169–180.

Germano, F., Jr. "Automatic Transaction Decomposition in a Distributed CODASYL Prototype System." Ph.D. diss., University of Pennsylvania, 1980.

———. "The Multiple-Schema Architecture of DSEED: A Distributed CODASYL Prototype System." *Proc. COMPCON80* (Fall 1980):383–391.

Hevner, A.R., and S.B. Yao. "Query Processing in a Distributed System." *Proc. Berkeley Workshop on Distributed Data Management and Computer Networks* (August 1978):91–107.

Wong. E. "Retrieving Dispersed Data from SDD-1: A System for Distributed Databases." *Proc. Berkeley Workshop on Distributed Data Management and Computer Networks* (May 1977):217–235.

Wong, E., and K. Youssefi. "Decomposition—A Strategy for Query Processing." *ACM Trans. on Database Systems* 1, no. 3 (September 1976):223–241.

Distributed Database Management Systems (Research Prototypes)

Bihan, J.L., C. Escalier, G. Lelann, W. Litwin, G. Gardarin, S. Sedillot, and L. Trielle. "SIRIUS: A French Nationwide Project on Distributed Data Bases." *Proc. VLDB* (October 1980):75–85.

Chang, E. "A Distributed Medical Data Base." *Computer Networks* 1, no. 1 (1976):33–38.

Chang, S.K., and W.H. Chen. "Structured Database Decomposition in Medical Information System Environment." *Proc. IEEE Computer Software and Applications Conference* (November 1977):71–79.

Held, G., M. Stonebraker, and E. Wong. "INGRES: A Relational Data Base System." *Proc. NCC 1975*, pp. 409–416.

Pliner, M., L. McGowan, and K. Spalding. "A Distributed Data Management System for Real Time Applications." *Proc. Berkeley Workshop on Distributed Data Management and Computer Networks* (May 1977):68–86.

Rothnie, J.B., Jr., et al. "Introduction to a System for Distributed Databases (SDD-1)." *ACM Trans. on Database Systems* 5, no. 1 (March 1980):1–17.

Rothnie, J.B., and N. Goodman. "An Overview of the Preliminary Design of SDD-1: A System for Distributed Databases." *Proc. Berkeley Workshop on Distributed Data Management and Computer Networks* (May 1977):39–57.

Stonebraker, M. "Retrospection on a Database System." *ACM Trans. Database Systems* 5, no. 2 (June 1980):225–240.

Stonebraker, M., and E. Neuhold. "A Distributed Data Base Version of INGRES."*Proc. Berkeley Workshop on Distributed Data Management and Computer Networks* (May 1977).

Stonebraker, M., E. Wong, P. Kreps, and G. Held. "The Design and Implementation of INGRES." *ACM Trans. on Database Systems* 1, no. 3 (September 1976):189–222.

Index

About the Author

Olin H. Bray is a senior consultant in the Data Management Technology Center at Control Data Corporation. He is currently working on the application of database methods to the CAD/CAM area, on the development of an engineering database management system, and on distributed database management systems. Previously, he was a principal systems design engineer at Sperry Univac, where he worked on database computer architectures and distributed database management. Prior to joining Sperry Univac, Mr. Bray worked on scientific applications, operating systems development, and as the MIS manager for a large health center. Mr. Bray received the B.S. in physics from the University of Alabama and the M.A. and M.B.A. from the University of Minnesota. Mr. Bray is a member of ACM, the IEEE Computer Society, and the CODASYL Systems Committee. He is also an ACM national lecturer on database computers, distributed database management systems, and CAD/CAM.